A Parisian in Xi'an

Published by
ACA Publishing Ltd.
University House
11-13 Lower Grosvenor Place,
London SW1W 0EX, UK
Tel: +44 (0)20 7834 7676
Fax: +44 (0)20 7973 0076
E-mail: info@alaincharlesasia.com
Web:www.alaincharlesasia.com
Beijing Office
Tel: +86(0)10 8472 1250
Fax: +86(0)10 5885 0639

Author: Deng Zhihui, Wang Junzhe
Editor: Caroline Hayes
Translator: Jiang Lin
Cover art: Daniel Li

Published by ACA Publishing Ltd in association
with the People's Publishing House

© 2014, by People's Publishing House, Beijing, China
ALL RIGHTS RESERVED. NO PART OF THIS
PUBLICATION MAY BE REPRODUCED IN MATERIAL FORM,
BY ANY MEANS, WHETHER GRAPHIC,
ELECTRONIC, MECHANICAL OR OTHER, INCLUDING
PHOTOCOPYING OR INFORMATION STORAGE, IN WHOLE OR IN PART, AND
MAY NOT BE USED TO PREPARE
OTHER PUBLICATIONS WITHOUT WRITTEN
PERMISSION FROM THE PUBLISHER.

The greatest care has been taken to ensure accuracy but the
publisher can accept no responsibility for errors or omissions, or
for any liability occasioned by relying on its content.

ISBN 978-1-910760-22-2

A catalogue record for *A Parisian in Xi'an* is available from
the National Bibliographic Service of the British Library.

Chinese editorial board of *A Parisian in Xi'an*

Directors: Deng Zhihui   Wang Junzhe

Deputy director: Wang Tianping

Members: (in alphabetical order)

    Jia Baojun   Zhang Baoning   Yang Chenguang   Lu Dong
    Guo Futing   Duan Hengchun   Wei Lanyu   Zhao Pei
    Geng Qiang   Gong Shijian   Guo Taichu   Li Tao
    Dang Xiaoxiang   Hou Xiaozhe   Su Yongqian   Liu Youyou
    Gong Yuwei   Ren Zhanfeng

Contents

Preface VI

Introduction   The China Dream of a French Man VII

Chapter 1   A French Expert in XISU 1
    1. The Department of German, French and Spanish Studies 4
    2. Cultivating XISU's French Faculty 7

Chapter 2   Dedicated Research of Chinese Culture 16
    1. Filling Gaps in Research on the Ming Dynasty (1368-1644) ... 21
    2. TCM, the Essence of Traditional Chinese Culture 27
    3. Worshipping Traditional Chinese Culture 32

Chapter 3   Building Sino-French Exchanges 37
    1. A Willing Envoy for Sino-French Cultural Exchanges 39
    2. Efforts to Subsidise Chinese Students in France 47
    3. Meticulous Care for Overseas Chinese Students in France .. 50
    4. An Inspiration to Chinese Students in France 52
    5. "My Roots are in Xi'an" 53

Chapter 4   Friendship with the Chinese People 58
    1. Adept at Making Friends 61
    2. Helping Others to Fulfill Their Dreams 68
    3. Cherished Priceless Friendship 70

	4. Considerate to Others 75
	5. Paternal Love for His Students 76
	6. Transmitted Great Love in 'Smiles' 78

Chapter 5 A Passion for China 81

	1. Service to the Chinese People 83
	2. Felt the Suffering of the Poor 84
	3. Heartfelt Help for Chinese Students in the Mountains 86
	4. The Warmth of the Chinese People 88
	5. Admiration for the Sacrifice of the Chinese People 92
	6. Deep Love for China 95

Chapter 6 Resting in Peace in His Second Home, China ... 104

	1. His Twilight Years 106
	2. His Last Days 111
	3. Fostering Later Generations 119

Epilogue Jean's Influence Continues Today 128

Compilers' Notes 137

Jean de Miribel – A Family History 141

Chronology – Jean de Miribel 160

Preface

I am humbled whenever I think of Jean de Miribel; I cannot help admiring his passionate character and his life. In France, he dedicated his time and energy to helping the poor and needy, even when France was under attack from a foreign aggressor. Everyone who has ever met him respects him as a sage, caring man, who valued human dignity and served others wholeheartedly.

He later lived in China. He arrived in Xi'an in September 1976, towards the end of the 'Cultural Revolution' (1966-1976), when only a few foreigners lived in China. He began to write his doctoral dissertation entitled *Asian Research on Provincial Administration and Civil Servants in the Ming Dynasty (1368-1644): Study of Shaanxi Province and Xi'an Prefecture*[1], working passionately on it for a decade. In addition to teaching in Xi'an International Studies University (XISU), he also devoted his time to encouraging young Chinese students to go to France, explore France, experience French culture and to learn French.

Jean de Miribel, the 'China hand', lived in China for almost 40 years. Now he is one of the leading figures stimulating the cultural dialogue and exchanges between Europe and China. Like his outstanding predecessors, he set us a good example. He once pointed out that cultural dialogue could provide young people the opportunity to get in touch with the world, even when in the greatest difficulties. His humanitarianism and his name will be remembered for ever in both China and France.

M. Maurice GOURDAULT-MONTAGNE
Ambassador of France in China
10 August 2016

---

[1] French title: *Administration Provinciale et Fonctionnaires Civils Au Temps des Ming (1368-1644): Etude de la Provice du Shaanxi et de la Prefecture de Xi'an (Recherches Asiatiques)*

Introduction

The China Dream of a French Man

Introduction

On an expanse of verdant lawn, on the Yanta campus of Xi'an International Studies University (XISU), in the southern suburbs of the ancient city of Xi'an, stands a monument built with a piece of black marble. Four big characters '耕耘友谊' (meaning 'cultivating friendship'), and an autograph of Cheng Andong, former governor of Shaanxi province, are engraved in the centre of the monument, with the portrait of an elderly French man inlaid in the upper right corner. He is Jean de Miribel, a French expert and an envoy of Sino-French cultural exchanges who dedicated the latter half of his life to China.

Speaking of Jean de Miribel, we have to shift our attention to the remote western world - Paris, the capital of the Republic of France. The world-renowned, historical city, built more than 1,400 years ago, is in the centre of the Paris Basin in northern France, with the gorgeous River Seine zig-zagging through it. It is a political, economic and cultural centre of not merely France but also the whole of western Europe. Paris is also a universally-recognised capital of culture and the centre of the European Enlightenment Movement and decorated by numerous world-famous landmark buildings such as the Eiffel Tower, Arc de Triomphe, the Louvre Museum and Notre Dame de Paris cathedral. Some great thinkers, writers and artists who influenced the world, such as Voltaire, Rousseau, Hugo, Balzac and Rodin, once lived and created works there. Paris is also a renowned capital of world art and the origin of impressionist art, ballet, film and the modern Olympic spirit. Jean de Miribel was born in the city on 5 August 1919.

The vast universe houses all the stars. As one of the stars of the solar system, the earth looks tiny and unbounded, soundless and full of gigantic power, it runs in its own orbit day and night without stopping, in all seasons. People living on the planet have also created abundant, colourful civilisations and culture with their own wisdom. Definitely, they have their own desires. Previously some attempted to conquer the eastern and western hemispheres by force and even dominate the whole earth with their power; nevertheless, the tiny earth is the shared homeland of mankind, and the people of all countries cherish peace and friendship, expect a harmonious co-existence and yearn for the world of universal harmony and love. For this reason, people of different nations or countries in different areas, either in the east or the west, and in different times, have tried their best and consecrated themselves in a bid to realise the best wishes of, and bridge the friendship between, the people in the east and west as the envoy of the eastern and western civilisations and culture. Jean de Miribel was a typical representative who devoted the latter half of his life to the friendship between China and France and their two peoples.

Jean de Miribel had an unusual life. He was born into the home of the gentry. His grandfather was one of the founding fathers of the French Air Force during World War I (WWI), his father was an aviator of the French Air Force during WWI and his elder female cousin once served as the confidential secretary of General Charles de Gaulle. During his schooldays, he lived in a house on a street in the 13th arrondissement in Paris, handed down from his ancestors. Just like all the other European buildings, the gate to his house looked stylish. The 13th arrondissement used to be one of the three Chinese quarters in Paris, enjoying great prestige in the whole of France, and also the earliest and the largest habitations of the Chinese in Paris. When he studied on a work-study basis in France in the early years, Zhou Enlai once lived in the unimpressive Hotel Neptune in Rue Godefroy near the Piazza Italia in the 13th arrondissement in Paris. It was also in the arrondissement that Zhou Enlai and his colleagues set up the headquarters of the Chinese Youth Communist Party in Europe, and the editorial department of *Red Light*, the theory journal of the party. The older generation of revolutionaries, such as Li Fuchun and Deng Xiaoping, had engaged in political activities there successively.

The first half of Jean de Miribel's life witnessed an enormous amount of twists and turns. When he was young, he studied at Lycée Montaigne and then Lycée Louis le Grand. He graduated from the Université Grenoble Alpes and got his bachelor's degree in history in January 1939. He was mobilised in the armed forces at Le Havre military camp in April 1940, and then studied in a school for officer cadets at Fontenay-le-Comte. At that time, World War II (WWII) was devastating the world, and he was captured as a soldier. After being released, he was demobilised from the army in September 1942. As his French friend, Pierre Rainero recollected, Jean de Miribel worked in the 13th arrondissement of Paris when he was young, gilding the edge of the New Year cards day after day and patiently listening to the hopes of his fellow workers. That experience significantly touched him. He once lived as a fisherman near the Pyrénées-Orientales and as a TV editor in a company in Montreuil. After WWII came to an end, he chose to travel all over the world, go to different countries, learn different languages and widely contact and know the beliefs and living conditions of the world's peoples. The moment he set foot on China, he

Introduction

told his Chinese friends that he had dreamed to travel throughout the whole world since middle school, and he yearned to go to China most, a mysterious, great remote country in the east. For that purpose, he came to Hong Kong on 15 March 1969, after working in Brazil. In Hong Kong he learned Cantonese, Mandarin and Chinese culture at New Asia College. Meanwhile, he patiently waited for the chance to get to mainland China. In 1975, the Consulate General of France in Hong Kong notified him that he might teach in Shanghai, although this venture failed for unknown reasons.

God always favours those of firm faith and tough determination. Jean de Miribel seemed to be born to come to China. In July 1976, Jean, a man of 57, finally had the chance. As a French historian, he was approved to visit Beijing, Dalian, Qingdao and Shanghai. His first trip to China coincided with the 1976 Tangshan earthquake. The hardships and sufferings brought by the earthquake to the Chinese civilians were deeply imprinted in his mind. In September 1976, Mao Zedong, a great leader of the Chinese people unfortunately passed away, leaving the whole nation in tremendous grief. Invited by the Chinese government, he had the honour to parade past the remains of Chairman Mao Zedong in Beijing, together with the ambassador of France to China. That special historical event exerted a huge impact on the French scholar who was almost 60 years old. Of course, the matter itself revealed the importance of his identity to be invited to parade past the body of Chairman Mao Zedong, a great man of worldwide influence, together with the ambassador of France to China. At that moment, he became the envoy of Sino-French cultural exchanges dispatched by the French government to China.

After the memorial ceremony for Mao Zedong, in line with the Sino-French cultural exchanges agreement, he could choose to work in Beijing, the capital city of China, or in Shanghai, a metropolis of China, in the capacity of an expert working in China. Although they were the cities boasting the best material conditions in China, he resolutely decided to work in Xi'an, an ancient city of harsh conditions in the north-west of China. His choice showed his wisdom, vision and far-sightedness as a historian. Xi'an, called Chang'an in the ancient times, was the origin of the Chinese civilisation and one of the four world-famous ancient capitals of civilisation. With a history of more than 3,100 years, it was situated in the centre of the Guanzhong Basin in Shaanxi, south of the towering Qinling Mountains and north of the surging Weihe river. Altogether 13 dynasties, including the Zhou dynasty (1046-249BC), the Qin dynasty (221-207BC), the Han dynasty (202BC-220AD) and the Tang dynasty (618-907AD) made Xi'an their capital. Besides, it was also the source of the ancient Silk Road. Historical sites are all over Xi'an, for instance, Banpo village (archaeological site near Xi'an) housing the Lantian men in the Paleolithic Age and the ancestors in the Neolithic Age, the Mausoleum of the First Qin Emperor, the terracotta soldiers and horses of the Qin dynasty, the Huaqing Palace in Mount Li, the Greater Wild Goose Pagoda and the Lesser Wild Goose Pagoda of the Tang dynasty, as well as the City Wall and the Forest of Stone Steles Museum of the Ming dynasty… All of them seem to compose a walking history book recording the vicissitudes of the Chinese nation. "The history of a city is the history of a nation." Like a giant magnet, the history and culture of Xi'an, an ancient city of China, strongly attracted the historian from the west.

Consequently, in line with the Sino-French cultural exchange agreement, Jean de Miribel was appointed by the Chinese Ministry of Education to teach French in Xi'an International Studies University (XISU) and concurrently studied Chinese history and culture. Since then, he put down roots there, settled, got on with his pursuits, worked and lived together with the teachers and students of XISU, and the ordinary people in Xi'an, until he passed away at the age of 96 and he now rests in peace in XISU. He contributed the latter half, almost 40 years of his life to XISU.

Chapter 1
A French Expert in XISU

Chapter 1

By September 1976, like other places in China, the ancient city of Xi'an had not recovered from the aftermath of the 'Cultural Revolution'. The slogans, seen everywhere in the streets and lanes, recounted the turmoil and unrest of the period, while the random, scattered shockproof sheds revealed the impact of the Tangshan earthquake in Xi'an. The natural and man-made disasters brought misery to the Chinese people who yearned for an end to the bitterness. Under such circumstances, Jean de Miribel flew into Xi'an on 21 September 1976 and became the first foreign expert at XISU (Xi'an International Studies University), the only foreign language university in north-west China at the time. At the airport and the university, he received a warm welcome from the leaders, teachers and students of the university.

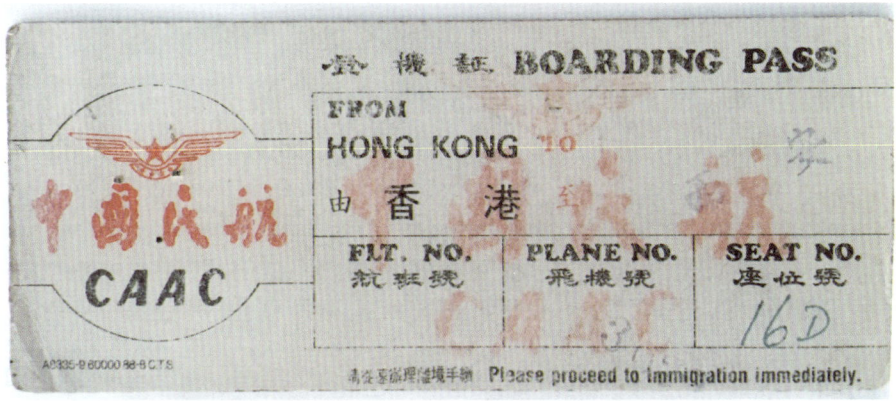

The boarding pass of Jean de Miribel, from Hong Kong to Xi'an, September 1976

An old Chinese proverb says: "People may survive natural disasters, but not man-made disasters." On 6 October 1976, the news that the 'Gang of Four' had been toppled spread through the country like wild fire. The elated Chinese people joyfully paraded in the streets, celebrating, to the accompaniment of gongs and drums. In a street in Xi'an, people spotted a tall foreigner in the XISU procession. Due to his curiosity and righteous nature, he quickly came to learn about the circumstances surrounding the Gang of Four. Like the Chinese, he waved colourful banners, excitedly shouted slogans and joined the celebrations. He was Jean de Miribel, a French expert, teaching in XISU. He immediately integrated himself into the ancient country, and its oriental civilisation, and established a deep affection for it.

1. The Department of German, French and Spanish Studies

Located in the ancient city of Xi'an, XISU was founded in 1951; its predecessor was Northwest Russian College. It was renamed in 1958 and became Xi'an International Studies University in 2006. The university is situated in the southern suburbs of the ancient city, close to such renowned historical and cultural sites as the Circular Mound Altar of the Sui and Tang dynasties, and the Qujiang pool. It faces the Temple of Thanksgiving, where Xuanzang oversaw the translation of Buddhist sutras, or religious literature. Standing on the campus, you can see the Greater Wild Goose Pagoda. There were many universities in China at the time, and although small in size, XISU was one of four foreign-language universities established under the new regime. It was popular with the party and the state. By the late 1970s, it had evolved to be a renowned foreign-language university, laying equal emphasis on the teaching of multiple languages, and was cultivating a myriad of language talents.

French was established as a specialty at the university in 1959, and the university began to enrol undergraduates in 1960. Nevertheless, its rapid development did not last long. When the Cultural Revolution broke out in 1966, enrolment for French, like other specialties at the university, stopped. The students went on strike and joined the revolution; classroom teaching was almost paralysed. The university began to enrol students from the peasant class, and then soldiers, in the later stages of the Cultural Revolution.

Mainland China had not opened its door to the outside world in the 1970s, and it was rare to see a blond foreigner in the street in a metropolis such as Xi'an. Not many foreign experts taught in the universities in Xi'an then; XISU had no more than 10 foreign teachers. Jean de Miribel was the only foreign teacher teaching French and his posting added vigour and vitality to the university. He provided timely help for the newly resumed specialty

Jean on the campus of XISU in 1979

of French. With fervent enthusiasm, he threw himself into rebuilding the teaching of French and succeeded in getting along very well with the teachers and students of the department. Other teachers and some students would come to his office and asked him all sorts of questions. The tall, foreign professor was liked by everyone, and was cordially known as 'Jean'.

As an expert teaching French, Jean gave elementary courses and lectures to French major students, such as French listening comprehension, French grammar, history and French culture, selected readings of French literature and French literary history. His teaching materials and lesson preparation cards show that he made careful preparation for the lectures. He meticulously wrote down the teaching objectives, lesson content, questions and answers in the class, in the lecture notes. He printed neatly so that the students could see more clearly in class. Many years later, the students could still remember the scenes in his class: a tall, slightly bald and big-nosed Frenchman, smiling sincerely, speaking slowly, who behaved gracefully, used simple words and told profound truths in his consummate lectures.

His teaching philosophy and methods were quite different from those of other teachers. He attached equal priority to cultivating the students' competence in the language, as to introducing the history and culture of France to his students due to his extensive knowledge. Hu Sishe, the current vice-chairman of the Chinese People's Association for Friendship with Foreign Countries, chose Jean's selected readings of French literature as a selective course. He recalled: "Jean's consummate explanation of the history and culture of France tremendously influenced me and I came to understand that learning French was not merely to master a language skill but also to study and research human science." Influenced by Jean's academic ideology, Hu Sishe assiduously studied French literature in Paris and attained a doctor's degree in French literature. When he later served as XISU president, he implemented Jean's spirit of human science in the university, which noticeably boosted the standing of XISU.

As a foreign expert, Jean taught students in accordance with their strengths and imperceptibly led the students to learn in his own way. Often, he patiently encouraged his students to find their own interest in learning, and was unwilling to measure students only through exams. At the end of each term, he did not set examinations, telling the perplexed students: "I'm not qualified to give you exams. You are all so excellent." It was his adeptness at teaching, his readiness to help, his erudition and his unique understanding of education that won him the respect of the students.

When the students were about to graduate each year, Jean would invite them individually to his office and talked to each of them for 10 minutes, to hear their feelings and experiences about the books they had studied, and their views on the history, culture and literature of France. Now we see that his caring teaching has influenced his students and friends, who adopted a French style of elegance, calmness and modesty.

Although he was usually lenient towards his students, he took important issues, points of principle, extremely seriously. Once, Liu Chunhui, one of Jean's students, applied to study in France and Jean invigilated the French evaluation exam for the university. During the exam, Jean's meticulous professionalism deeply impressed Liu Chunhui. When Liu Chunhui recalled the event 20 years later, he reflected: "I had originally planned to cheat, but it was blasphemy to the upright personality of Jean." Jean's seriousness and responsibility for work were imprinted in the mind of many people. Jiang Xiaomin, who worked in the office of foreign affairs of XISU, recalled Jean with deep affection: "I gradually sensed that although Jean is a Frenchman, he is not characterised by the romance and casualness of some French men, but more by the seriousness and persistence of a French scholar. From him, I've experienced what the genuine spirit of France is: that is, the marriage of romance and seriousness and the unity of art and harmony."

Jean's wisdom and erudition rapidly won widespread commendation and respect of the students. His lectures attracted numerous students of the School of Foreign Languages and even many students from other departments came to see his elegant demeanour, and to admire him. As Jia Zhenfan, a German major student of XISU, recalled: "I met Jean at the meet-and-greet of the freshmen of the School of German, French and Spanish Studies of XISU in 1978. The thunderous applause and laughter of the French majors drew me to listen to the passionate speech of the French expert. Although I couldn't understand a single French sentence, I could still sense the benevolent affection, wisdom, humour and personal charm of the erudite elder, and the beautiful melody of his speech in French, from the enthusiasm around me."

As a foreign teacher of French, he paid more attention to cultivating the students' sense of language and inspiring them to apply the language in ordinary life, in his teaching. It deeply influenced his students. Huang Chuangen was one of the first students majoring in French at XISU after the reform of the college entrance examination system. He studied French grammar under Jean and, after graduating, taught in the university. With Jean's influence and help, he studied the method of French teaching in a university in Lyon, France and devoted himself to researching the teaching method after he returned home. In 2015, he finished writing *Analysis of French Grammar in Practice*[1] and signed a publishing contract with Commercial Press. As a student of Jean's, he originally expected to present the book to his teacher, but sadly Jean passed away before its publication. That unfulfilled wish became a stabbing pain in the heart of Huang Chuangen forever.

2. Cultivating XISU's French Faculty

Jean began to teach in China as the Cultural Revolution was coming to an end and when there was much to be done. The decade of havoc brought innumerable losses to state education and foreign language education suffered the most. At that time, the French department did not have teaching materials and electronic teaching equipment. There was a lack of original newspapers and magazines in French. The teachers and students could not read original French works, watch original French films or have basic reference books, all indispensable for teaching and researching in French, nor could they cooperate or set up exchanges with foreign universities.

Jean kept all these difficulties in mind and tried whatever measures and channels were necessary to solve them, one by one. With the help of the French embassy in China, he provided the department with some books and data it badly needed for teaching and scientific research. He helped set up a French library and subscribed to *Le Monde* on behalf of the department. Taking the opportunity of going to Hong Kong, he spent his limited salary buying dozens of rare, precious tape recorders, as audio-visual teaching aids, and improved the listening and speaking levels of the teachers and students of the School of Foreign Languages. Each year, when he returned to his family in France, Jean would purchase books and materials that were urgently needed for teaching and research at the university, at his own expense.

---

[1] **French title:** *Analyse de la Grammaire Française dans la Pratique*

Professor Shen Youtai, former vice president of XISU, once said: "Jean accompanied the Chinese people as they underwent their most difficult period, and brought original French films to the French teachers and students of XISU in the years when the model opera prevailed." The teachers and students of XISU in the early 1980s knew that the university lacked cultural and entertainment activities, and a film screening on the area in front of the university auditorium every Saturday evening provided welcome entertainment. Most of the audience watching the films then may not have known that original, classic French films such as *The Lady of the Camellias, The Three Musketeers, Notre Dame de Paris, Les Miserables, The Red and the Black* and *La Chartreuse de Parme*, were specially borrowed by Jean from the French embassy. As the films played, the teacher provided simultaneous translation, standing beneath the screen with a microphone in his hand while the audience watched with great pleasure. What a crowd under the starry sky! Although the teacher's translation did not follow the captions, the viewers were still immersed in the film's story. Each time, Jean would stand behind the audience and watch the films silently, together with other teachers and students; he still wore a smile on his face, and was graceful and calm. Sometimes, the students of Shaanxi Normal University, which was separated from XISU by just a wall, came to watch the foreign films in the School of Foreign Languages. Professor Zhang Baoning, now teaching in XISU, used to be one of the students of Shaanxi Normal University who watched films, free of charge, in the School of Foreign Languages of XISU. Speaking of the scenes in those years, he recalled how often he would run across to XISU to watch 'scrounged', dubbed French films. Another student, Ren Zhanfang, who majored in German, recollected that a heavy fog fell very suddenly when they were happily watching a film. Although the image from the screen was not bright and clear, the audience was still reluctant to leave and stayed to listen to the end of the film, still in high spirits.

As a well-travelled, cultural and educational expert of the United Nations (UN), with a global vision, Jean keenly felt that opportunities for further education and exchanges overseas must be created for teachers to fundamentally improve the teaching standards of the Chinese universities, and especially teachers of schools of foreign languages. Nevertheless, the early 1980s were extremely difficult for XISU. Opportunities, and the funding, to go abroad were scarce. Jean was concerned, and created a way to bring about intercollegiate exchanges with foreign universities. It has become pivotal today for Chinese universities to carry out cross-border intercollegiate exchanges, and most domestic, Chinese universities have established partnerships with their foreign counterparts. Nonetheless, Jean's idea, in the initial stage of reform, seemed to be audacious. With the support of the directors of the university, Jean repeatedly contacted foreign universities, seeking the chance of cooperation. In 1980, he initially connected with the University of Paris VIII, with the help of his old friend Madam Rua, a French expert on Lu Xun. The two universities took the lead in establishing an intercollegiate partnership. In doing so, XISU established a model for its domestic counterparts. In the summer holidays, the Ministry of Higher Education organised for the representatives of 10 foreign-language universities to investigate the project in France. The leaders of XISU nominated Wang Kejian, the head of the Department of German, French and Spanish, as a delegate to visit Paris. XISU and the University of Paris VIII signed an intercollegiate exchange agreement, thanks to Jean's help. When Wang Kejian went through the formalities at the Ministry of Higher Education before the visit, the comrades at the ministry congratulated him, saying: "Your university is the sixth nationwide to establish ties for international exchanges. How lucky you are!"

Jean and his friends at Christmas, 1990

Jean and his students participating in the October 1992 anniversary of the founding of XISU

Jean, Wang Liqun, Li Jianguo and Liu Chunhui accompanying their friends to tour the Qianling mausoleum in 1992

A group photo of Jean and the family of Yu Wu and Zhu Zuhua in June 1993

Chapter 1

Jean and his friends in his home in the foreign faculty residence of XISU in 1994

When the agreement was signed, Wang Kejian was appointed by University of Paris VIII as a guest professor to teach in the department of Chinese language and literature. In return, Professor Vincent Vidal, department head of political economy of the University of Paris VIII, was appointed by XISU as an expert to teach in China. During his work in the University of Paris VIII, Wang Kejian met some Swiss friends, including Professor Jean Francois Billeter, department head of Chinese language and literature of the University of Geneva, introduced by Jean de Miribel. He also later signed an agreement to establish an intercollegiate partnership with the University of Geneva and the University of Lausanne on behalf of XISU.

As a result of exchange relationships established by Jean de Miribel, XISU dispatched more than 10 teachers to the aforementioned foreign universities for further study in those years, which significantly improved the teachers professionally and the teaching quality of the French department at XISU. It is no exaggeration to say that it was Jean that made a pioneering contribution to the growth of the French faculty at XISU.

In addition to teaching the students, Jean also gave various lectures to other teachers, in a drive to boost teaching standards. Liang Jialin, a teacher in the reference room of the French department, was also helped by Jean. Almost every time before he returned to France, Jean asked Liang Jialin whether he could do something, buy him some books, for instance. For some time, Liang Jialin had been translating the works of American writer Hugh Lofting and wanted to translate all his original works which were unavailable in China. Jean was returning to France, and came as usual to ask Liang Jialin whether he needed some help. Liang Jialin wrote down the title of the book he needed. On his return from France after the summer holidays, Jean brought a thick book to Liang Jialin; it was *W.Somerset Maugham Collected Short Stories* which had nothing to do with the book he needed. Jean explained: "I asked my friend, a writer, to buy you the book. She said the book you needed was written by a lesser-known writer and you should translate the works of Maugham who is much more famous in China." Liang Jialin could only explain to Jean: "Maugham is a Nobel prize winner. He is so famous that I'm not qualified to translate his books into Chinese. I have to select the book suitable for me." Jean nodded in subtle embarrassment and left waving his hands helplessly. One year later, Jean returned to France and, when he came back to China, brought Liang Jialin the requested Hugh Lofting book. Years later, Liang Jialin translated all the works of Hugh Lofting, including the one brought back by Jean. Now Liang Jialin is a prestigious translator.

Jean had taught in XISU for eight years and retired when his contract expired in July 1984. The Chinese Ministry of Education approved his application to remain in Xi'an. He still lived on the Yanta campus of XISU and began to throw himself into academic research. With the help of his friends, including former curator of XISU Lu Dong, French professor Guo Taichu, Sun Zhenjiao from Xi'an Friendship Hospital and Ma Xi from Xi'an Medical University, Jean completed such works as *Asian Research on Provincial Administration and Civil Servants in the Ming Dynasty (1368-1644): Study of Shaanxi Province and Xi'an Prefecture*, *Medical Practices in China - From Traditional Medicine to Surgery*[2], *Epidemic Diseases in Imperial China*[3] and *The Wisdom of China — Another Sort of Culture*[4].

On 5 May 1995, XISU appointed Jean a lifelong, honourary professor, for his contribution to the teaching of French, establishing the French faculty, and the undertaking of Sino-French cultural exchanges. At the appointment ceremony, Jean delivered an ebullient speech:

---

[2] French title: *Pratiques Medicales en Chine - de la Médecine Traditionnelle à la Chirurgie*
[3] French title: *Les Maux Épidémiques dans l'Empire Chinois* by Lu Dong, Ma Xi and François Thann (pen name of Jean de Miribel)
[4] French title: *Sagesse Chinoise: une Autre Culture*

Chapter 1

Dear President Sun Tianyi,

Dear friends,

It is my privilege and pleasure to receive the lifelong title of honourary professor, conferred on me by XISU. My sincerest gratitude should go to President Sun Tianyi, Secretary Zhang Fenghai and my fellow teachers and students, who have helped me. I sincerely believe that the true value of the honour is to mark the deep friendship nurtured over a long time.

Jean and former presidents of XISU, Zhong Qiqing and Sun Tianyi

Zhong Qiqing, former president of XISU, presenting the honourary certificate to Jean

I feel fortunate to have worked and lived in XISU for the second half of my life. For 18 years, I've seen the gigantic changes of both XISU and China as a whole. I can say that I am a witness to China's reform, progress and development. If we say China represents the trend of development of the 'third world', then I have a hunch that China will lead world development and play an increasingly bigger role in world affairs in the next 25 years.

Thanks to the support and help of the leaders and friends in XISU, I succeeded in my efforts for Sino-French cultural exchanges. I found that XISU boasts many conditions and opportunities favourable for these Sino-French cultural exchanges. All the French visitors in Xi'an who have been to XISU, have been influenced by the Chinese culture and found their trip here rewarding.

Certificate from XISU, appointing Jean a lifelong, honourary professor

Jean, Zhang Xiaohui, Zhang Chi and Liu Chunhui in the summer of 2010

Chapter 1

I really feel I have been blessed. It can be said that I am both a teacher and a student in Xi'an, incessantly learning and discovering such a great, abundant and historic civilisation. How many people in the world are lucky enough to work and live in the cradle of Chinese culture today?

I'd like to take the opportunity of this ceremony to show my heartfelt thanks to my dearest friends and the teachers of the French department, especially President Sun Tianyi, for your help, care and trust in me for 18 years! As an old Chinese saying goes: "Friendship lasts forever". I wish us a permanent friendship!

Chapter 2
Dedicated Research of Chinese Culture

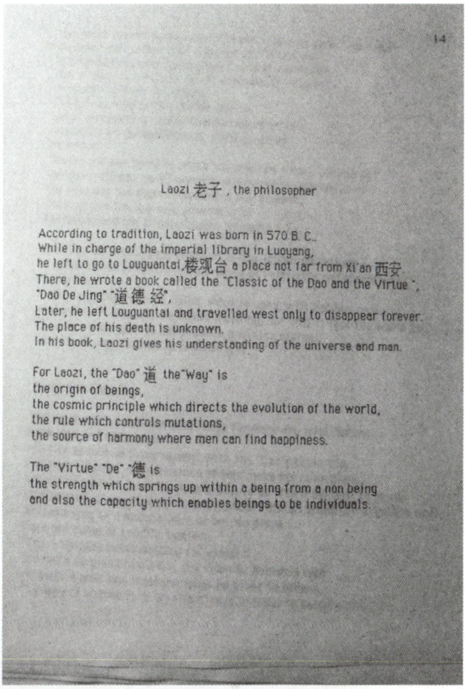

Laozi 老子, the philosopher

According to tradition, Laozi was born in 570 B.C..
While in charge of the imperial library in Luoyang,
he left to go to Louguantai, 楼观台 a place not far from Xi'an 西安.
There, he wrote a book called the "Classic of the Dao and the Virtue ",
"Dao De Jing" "道德经",
Later, he left Louguantai and travelled west only to disappear forever.
The place of his death is unknown.
In his book, Laozi gives his understanding of the universe and man.

For Laozi, the "Dao" 道 the "Way" is
the origin of beings,
the cosmic principle which directs the evolution of the world,
the rule which controls mutations,
the source of harmony where men can find happiness.

The "Virtue" "De" 德 is
the strength which springs up within a being from a non being
and also the capacity which enables beings to be individuals.

As soon as he set foot on mainland China, Jean became interested in everything Chinese, especially traditional Chinese culture. He adopted a Chinese name, Mi Ruizhe. However, first he would have to learn to read and write the Chinese characters, to genuinely understand the Chinese culture. The Chinese characters seem obscure to westerners, accustomed to the Latin script and alphabet. The Chinese characters seem puzzling to many westerners.

Before he came to mainland China, Jean had studied and lived in Hong Kong for many years and could communicate in Cantonese and Mandarin. After coming to mainland China, Jean became increasingly interested in the Chinese culture. He often told his friends: "China and Chinese morality and education left the best impression on me. Xi'an used to be the capital city of more than 10 dynasties, including the Zhou dynasty, the Qin dynasty, the Han dynasty and the Tang dynasty. It houses so many imperial mausoleums and innumerable miracles and secrets. It is a good place for me to study, as I like history very much!" For his research into Chinese culture, Jean was determined to continue to learn Chinese when he was in his fifties.

Jean signing his Chinese name '米睿哲'

Chapter 2

Jean researching a project

Some works written by Jean

Geng Qiang (left), Yang Chenguang (centre) and Jean

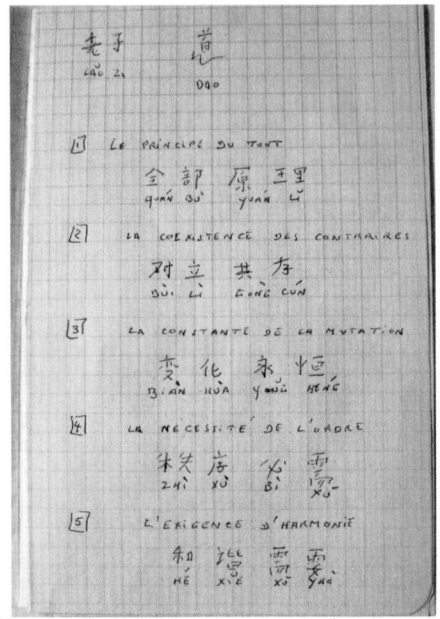

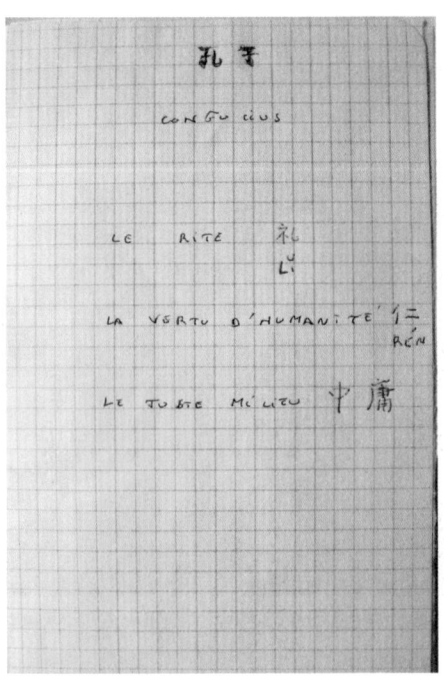

Jean's manuscript on traditional Chinese culture

Chapter 2

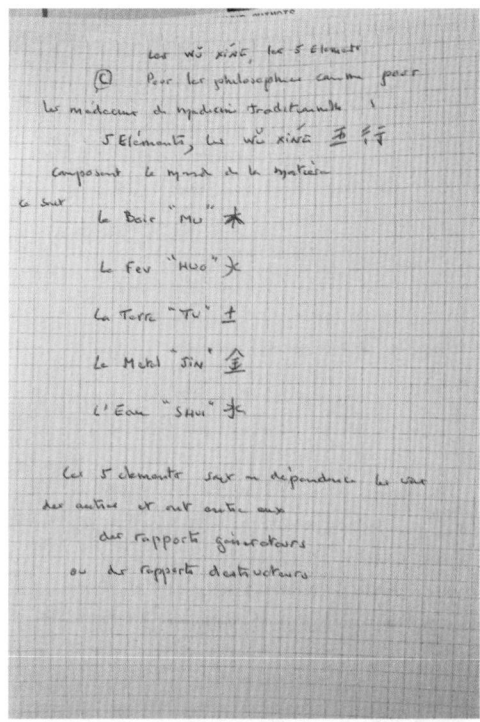

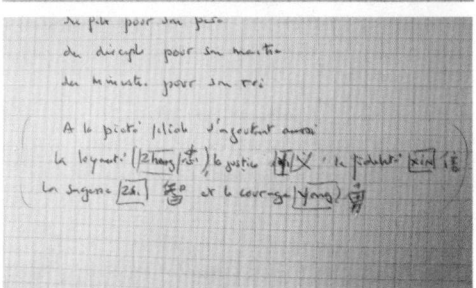

Another of Jean's hand-written manuscripts on traditional Chinese culture

One of Jean's first friends in XISU was Lu Dong. As they were colleagues and neigbours, Lu Dong was tasked with teaching Jean Chinese. When he encountered difficulties, Jean would always seek advice from Lu Dong. Among Jean's effects was a particularly striking copy of his manuscript. On a piece of clean, quadrille paper were the Chinese characters '中国' '北京' '西安' neatly written and marked with corresponding pinyin. Exceedingly talented at languages, Jean was proficient in four languages and interested in the local dialects. He picked up Cantonese when he lived in Hong Kong and some Shanghai dialect during his tour of Shanghai. Thanks to his diligence, he made rapid progress in learning Mandarin in Xi'an. When with friends, he would make jokes in the Guanzhong dialect, in a strong French accent.

1. Filling Gaps in Research on the Ming Dynasty (1368-1644)

Jean was in his sixties in the early 1980s. He did not hurry to return to France after he retired from XISU, but decided to continue to live in Xi'an, hoping to concentrate on studying the traditional Chinese culture. Years later, he successively completed *Asian Research on Provincial Administration and Civil Servants in the Ming Dynasty (1368-1644): Study of Shaanxi Province and Xi'an Prefecture*, *The Epidemic Evils in China* and *The Wisdom of China – Another Sort of Culture*. The contents covered

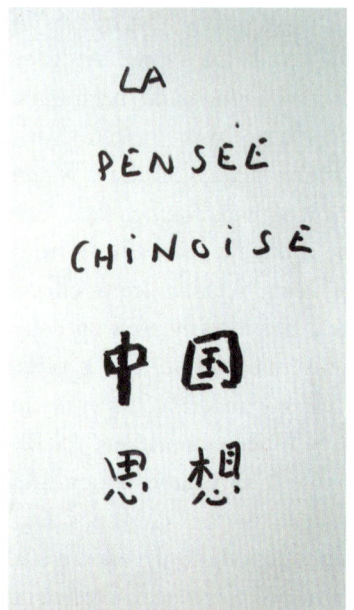

An example of Jean's original handwriting

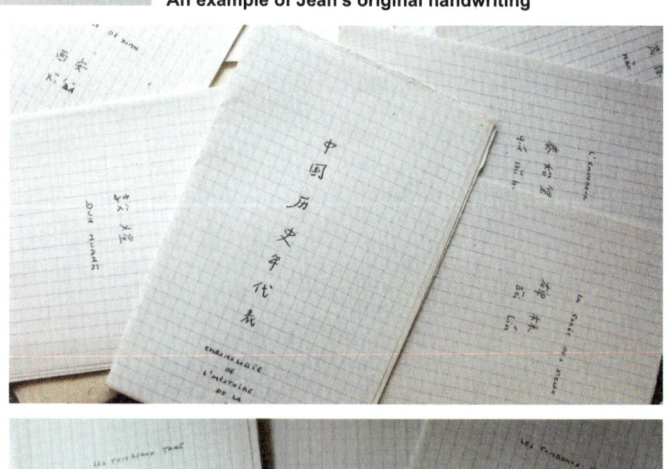

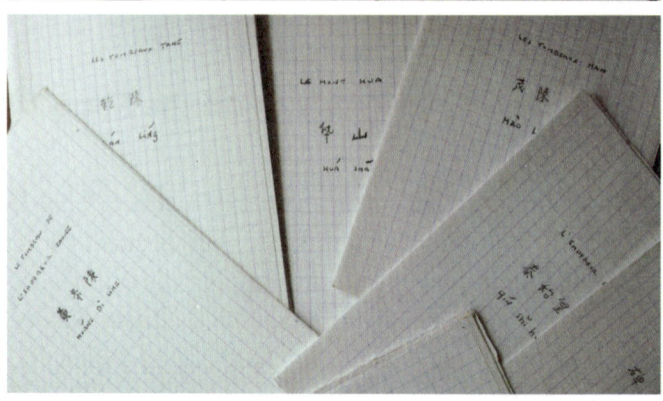

Jean's manuscript, introducing traditional Chinese culture and famous scenic spots and historical sites in Xi'an to his French friends

many aspects, such as Chinese history, traditional Chinese medicine, and philosophy. Of these, he exerted most energy in completing *Asian Research on Provincial Administration and Civil Servants in the Ming Dynasty (1368-1644): Study of Shaanxi Province and Xi'an Prefecture*, in 1985. Jean was stimulated to write the book when his friend, Léon Vandermeersch, a prestigious French Sinologist, paid him a visit.

Jean and Lu Dong preparing for a dissertation presentation, September 1985

The International Symposium on the History of the Ming and Qing Dynasties in China was held in Tianjin in August 1980. Sinologists from many countries, including Japan, the US, Australia, Germany and Switzerland, were invited to attend. Only French scholars were not invited to attend, not because of academic prejudice against France, but because France did not have any experts on the Ming and Qing dynasties in China. It upset French Sinologists Léon Vandermeersch and Jacques Gernet tremendously. How could France enhance its research on Chinese history? Léon Vandermeersch thought of Jean de Miribel, his old friend teaching far away in China. He paid a visit to Jean, and hoped that he could take advantage of his position, working in China, to research Chinese history. As his friends had hoped, Jean

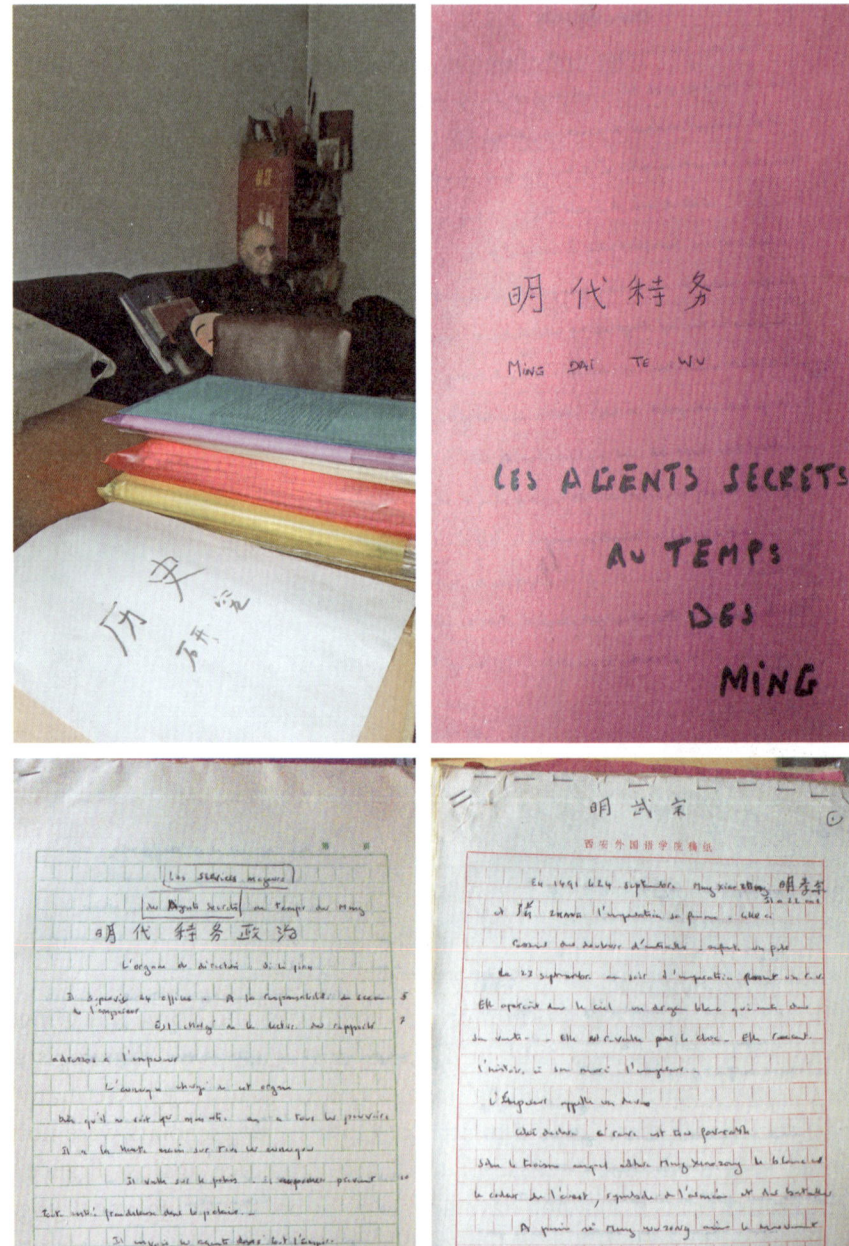

Jean's original manuscript of his research on the history of the Ming dynasty

enthusiastically agreed. At the suggestions of his Chinese friends, Jean quickly decided on the focus of his research: provincial officials and the civil service system in the Ming dynasty. He invited Lu Dong to join him in the research.

Every day, during breaks, Jean went to the neighbouring Shaanxi Normal University, and looked up historical data on the Ming and Qing dynasties in the library. To obtain first-hand materials, Jean and Lu Dong conducted field research in almost every county in Shaanxi. It was not until 1985 that Jean finished his 280,000-word project. His stacked research manuscripts were taller than a person. He had taken meticulous statistics of the appearances, ages, deportment and temperaments of the officials of the Ming dynasty, illustrating the precision and care of the French Sinologist. When completed, the work caused great excitement in China, as reported in *Shaanxi Daily*:

> *Asian Research on Provincial Administration and Civil Servants in the Ming Dynasty (1368-1644): Study of Shaanxi Province and Xi'an Prefecture* was completed by French Professor Jean de Miribel of XISU in May. The long, literary, academic paper of up to 700 pages (Chinese edition) was written by Jean in his spare time during his six years of teaching at XISU. During his research, Jean referenced up to 100 sorts of Chinese and foreign books, including the *History of Ming Dynasty* comprising 320 volumes, with the help of Lu Dong, Guo Taichu and Bi Shengmei, all lecturers at XISU.
>
> At the official invitation of the famous Paris Diderot University, Lu Dong and Guo Taichu, who helped compile *Asian Research on Provincial Administration and Civil Servants in the Ming Dynasty (1368-1644): Study of Shaanxi Province and Xi'an Prefecture*, would become members of the dissertation examination board, held in Paris in October.
>
> It was learned that the dissertation would fill the gaps in French research on Chinese history, and serve as a model for Chinese and foreign scholars to jointly discuss the history of human civilisation. It was rare in the history of Chinese-foreign cultural exchanges, that Chinese teachers and prestigious French Sinologists and historians jointly composed the examination board.

Later, the 'Detailed Outline of Newspapers of Capital, Provinces and Municipalities' column, in *People's Daily*, reprinted the report on the publication of the book.

Before the doctoral dissertation presentation, Jean told Lu Dong: "My mother is over 90 years old and in ill health, but let me tell you, she has been waiting for the day of my presentation, and she wants to attend." As predicted, his mother passed away after she was able to attend her son's dissertation presentation. Photos of Jean at the presentation in France, in October 1985, were treasured in Lu Dong's home. As the dissertation filled gaps in French Sinologist research on the history of the Ming dynasty in China, Jean received a doctoral degree, conferred by Paris Diderot University. This was the first of its kind for research on the history of the Ming dynasty in China. For the dissertation presentation, several hundreds of visitors attended. Even the famous *Le Monde* of France wrote an epoch-making report on the doctoral dissertation. Experts evaluated the dissertation highly, and unanimously agreed to award Jean the 'top

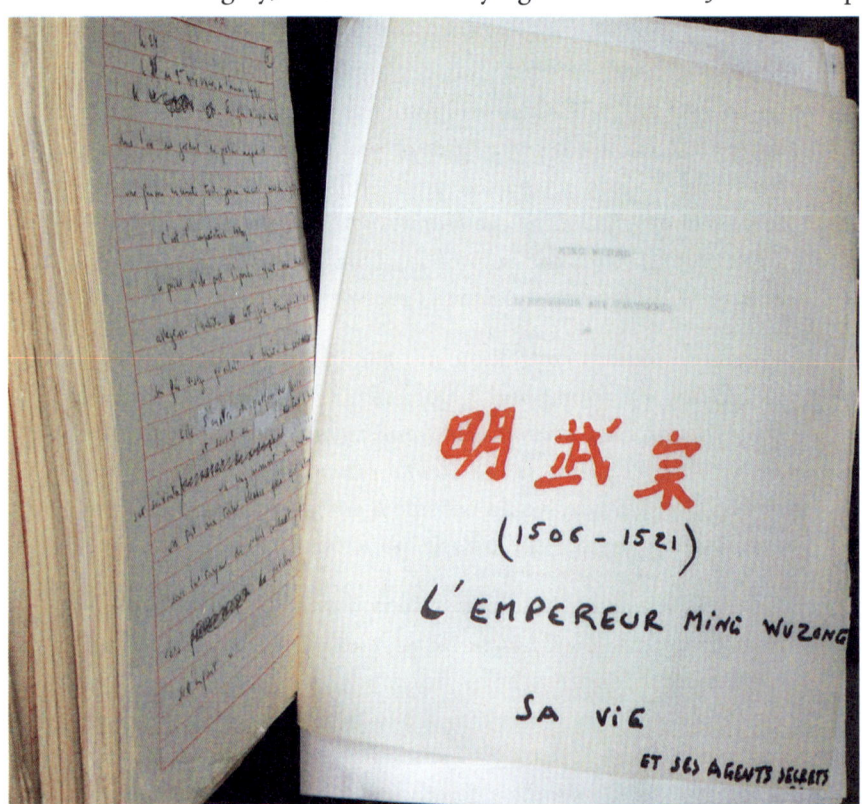

Jean's original manuscript of his research on the history of the Ming dynasty

grade'. Léon Vandermeersch, one of the dissertation reviewers, pointed out: "Jean de Miribel's research is original and valuable. It is the first successful research done in such a manner in mainland China and hence boasts great significance and value." The cultural significance and role of the dissertation in the history of Sino-French cultural exchanges should not be underestimated, in terms of tolerance, allowing a foreign expert to conduct research, and as a sign of China, after its reform, in opening up. The dissertation was later translated by Professors Guo Taichu, Zhang Shangci and Jiang Zihua into Chinese. Former President Sun Tianyi of XISU wrote in the preface of the Chinese edition: "It is, so far, the first special research on the north-western area of China in the Ming dynasty. No one before has made a multi-perspective and multi-dimensional analysis like this, on the administrative management, and the work, lives, personalities and hobbies of the civil officials of the provincial governments of the Ming dynasty. What's especially valuable is the statistical data and tables, which have brought to life the social environment in those years, and enabled readers to know and recognise specific historical facts. Mr. Jean de Miribel is adept in writing the historical material in a clear, elegant and attractive style. His clear knowledge of the organised, advanced administrative system in ancient China is evident throughout, and reminds me of the influence of China's civil service system on Europe, and its attraction for Europe three or four centuries ago." That dissertation brought the uniqueness and brilliance of the Chinese culture to more French Sinologists. It was soon afterwards, under the influence of Jean, that another French Sinologist, Hugues de Thé, enthusiastically began researching Chinese traditional calligraphy and Jiangyong female script, in Hunan.

2. TCM, the Essence of Traditional Chinese Culture

Traditional Chinese Medicine (TCM) has been of central interest to western missionaries and Sinologists. As early as the mid 17th century, a Polish missionary, named Michael Boym (1612-1659), introduced Chinese medical books, such as *The Medical Classic of the Yellow Emperor* and *Pulse Classic*, to the west. He wrote *The Key to Medicine*, on the subject, and initiated western research on TCM. Later Sinologists were all significantly interested in the mysterious, oriental, medical knowledge. TCM also intrigued Jean de Miribel.

In the ancient city of Xi'an, many people knew Jean's stories but only a few knew of his passion for, and his research into the history of, TCM.

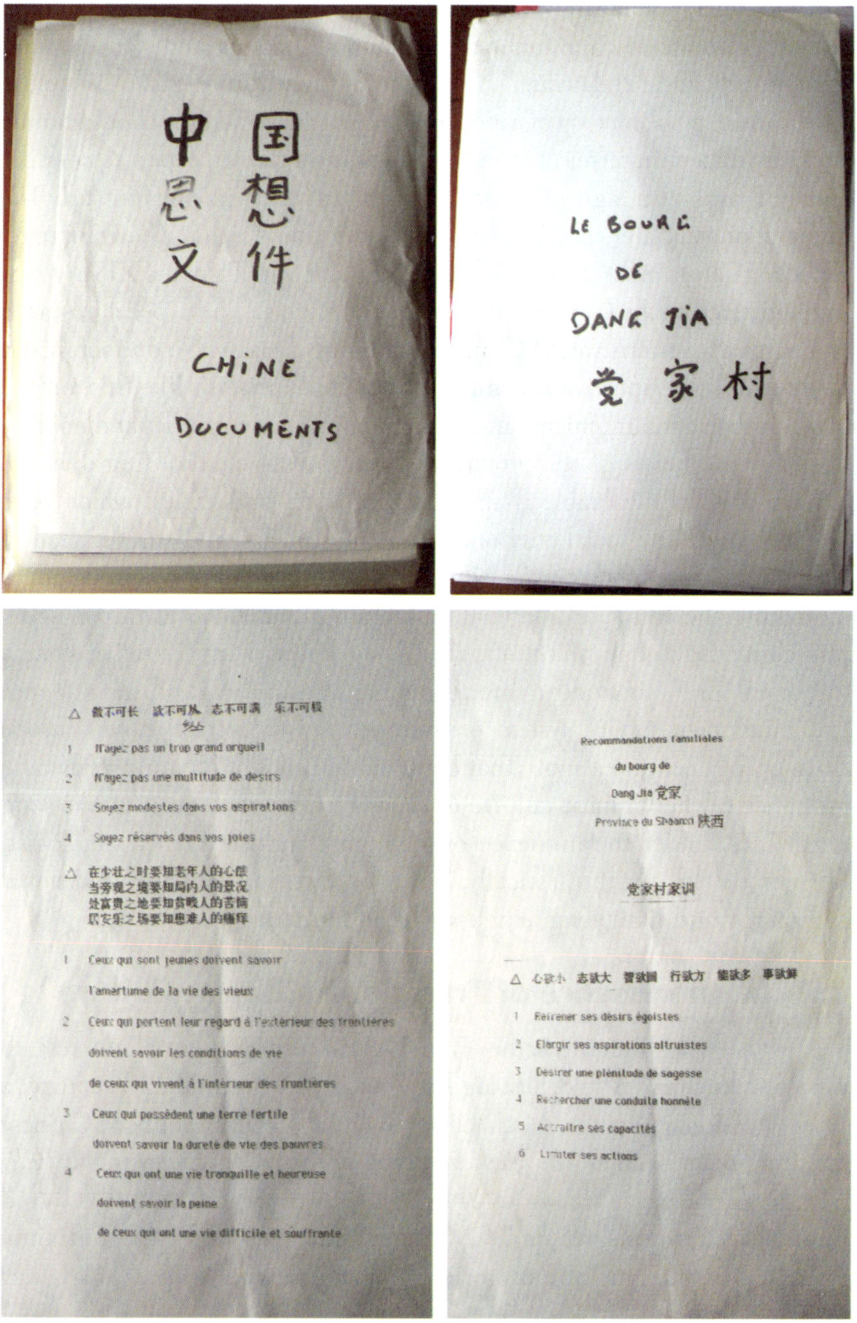

French text, introducing the traditional culture of the Dangjia village to his French friends, translated by Jean

As a scholar, Jean did not specialise in medicine initially. He had studied at the University of Grenoble Alpes when he was younger, and obtained a national doctoral degree from the Paris Diderot University for his research on the history of the Ming and Qing dynasties of China. For many, Jean's academic interest shifting from history to TCM seemed somewhat abrupt.

As a matter of fact, Jean became attracted to TCM gradually. In the late 1970s, not long after he arrived in Xi'an, he visited the Forest of Stone Steles Museum, which was hosting an exhibition of the history of medical science in the Tang dynasty. The fact that Chinese people prized TCM literature, and had respected the TCM doctors for more than 1,300 years, profoundly influenced the Frenchman and he decided to research the history of TCM. There was also another issue that aroused Jean's fervent interest in TCM. Soon after he came to Xi'an, he was admitted to the Shaanxi Provincial People's Hospital, with a disease which was diagnosed and quickly cured by a TCM doctor at the hospital. It further increased Jean's interest in TCM. Up until that point, TCM was viewed as a pseudo-science and incompatible with modern medical science; a view that prevailed in both China and the west, influenced by the advance of science. Through his personal experience and observation, Jean discovered that TCM was based on knowledge, and was a precious heritage contributed by Chinese culture to the whole world. Jean also carefully observed and emulated the clinical areas of TCM, such as acupuncture, moxibustion and taking a patient's pulse. All of which combined to leave a deep impression on him and motivated him to further study and research TCM.

To research the history of TCM, Jean invited then-President Yang Zhen, of Xi'an Hospital of Traditional Chinese Medicine, to give a lecture on TCM each weekend for the next two years. His studies meant Jean became aware that TCM was far more complicated than he previously imagined. For instance, the 24-pulse diagnosis method can only really be mastered after a long period of practice. After systematically learning about TCM, Jean and colleagues at Xi'an jointly researched the history of TCM. Among Jean's effects, were ancient books and his original manuscripts to research TCM culture. Its TCM terminology, and the Yin Yang chart of Tai Ji, meticulously transcribed by Jean, illustrate the respect and care of a French Sinologist for TCM.

After years of effort, Jean and his colleagues co-published academic studies, such as *The Epidemic Evils in China* and *Medical Practices in China-From Traditional Medicine to Surgery*. Jean believed that the western world generally misunderstood TCM and he, a Sinologist sojourning in China for so many years, was obliged to introduce it to TCM, to begin a dialogue on TCM and western medical science. *The Wisdom of China*[1] co-authored by Jean and another French Sinologist, also introduced TCM. In the process of his research, Jean gradually came to realise that TCM and the ideology of the Chinese were closely tied from a historical perspective; a foreigner would find great difficulties in understanding the Chinese without any knowledge of TCM.

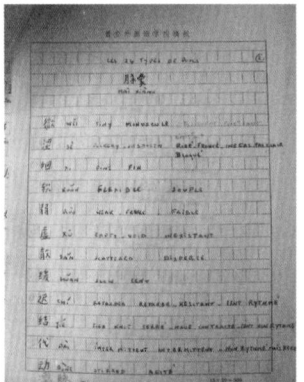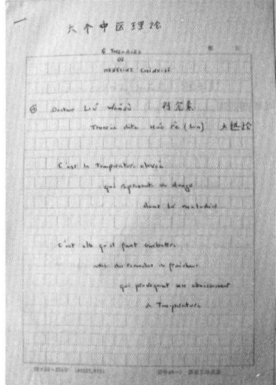

Jean's manuscripts, during his research of TCM

Despite its long history, the TCM culture was in danger of being marginalised day by day by a materialistic society. Until his death, Jean chiefly chose to consult TCM doctors to maintain his health. His painful, chronic illnesses were eliminated by concentrations of medicinal ingredients, acupuncture and moxibustion therapy, as well as massage treatment prescribed and administered by TCM doctors. Realising what lay ahead, Jean was disturbed when he personally experienced TCM. In a discussion with Doctor Yang Chenguang of Shaanxi Province Hospital of Traditional Chinese Medicine, Jean anxiously said:

"The troubles ahead for TCM will not be the ideology of the Chinese people, but more probably, money. The druggists will encourage doctors to prescribe their drugs rather than apply the TCM method, weakening its standing; additionally, TCM doctors may not know the chemical components and pharmacologic effects of western medicine as well

---

[1] **French title: *Sagesse Chinoise***

as TCM's taste and properties. The present development of modern medicine has a close relation with business, while TCM places more importance on the value of doctors, their ideology, and its vital medical ethics of saving the patient's money. Some doctors even diagnose and treat patients at their own expense. It is so great! So in the modern times, where economic interests are uppermost, TCM development will be restricted.

"To maintain the traditions of TCM requires resistance to excessive commercialisation. TCM must not be allowed to pursue money at the expense of destroying TCM. Once destroyed, TCM would be difficult to recover. The destruction of TCM would mean the destruction of the roots of China. It would surely be a great tragedy. TCM will not make much money, however, whether it makes money or not, TCM should be supported, since it is as valuable as the history of China. Researching history will not make a lot of money, but it doesn't mean history is not important. 'Money talks' is the ideology cherished by the westerners. You are Chinese, not western, and you should carry on your own traditions. It is hoped that high-calibre TCM groups can agree with this view, and echo such appeals."

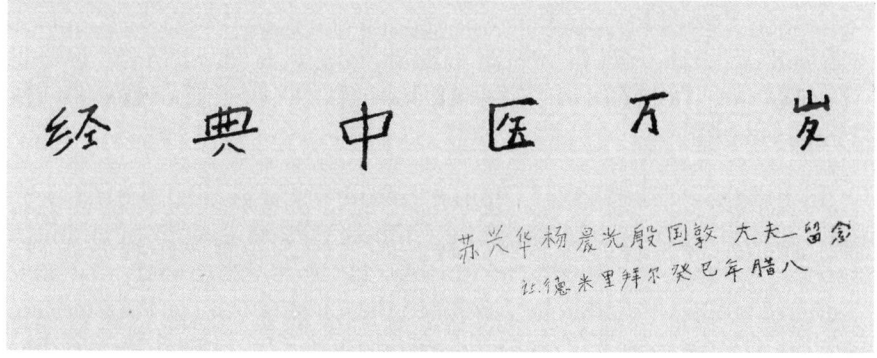

Jean's calligraphy written in his own handwriting '经典中医万岁' (Long live the classic TCM) for his TCM friends in 2013

In Jean's opinion, the Chinese should "carry on the traditions of TCM and resist excessive commercialisation" and "support the inheritance and development of TCM". On another occasion, Jean even proposed that China should establish TCM awards of the level of the Nobel Prize in physiology or medicine, in a drive to encourage worldwide research and study on TCM. Even if Jean's suggestions are not acted upon, the concerns of a senior Frenchman about TCM are still worthy of serious reflection by every Chinese person.

3. Worshipping Traditional Chinese Culture

Before his death, Jean lived in an old-style building, in the north-eastern corner of the Yanta campus of XISU, covered with Sinomenium acutum. His house was not big, approximately 60m². It contained just one living room and a hall. The university did offer to change it to a bigger, newer one, but he declined, saying: "My noble character lights up the humble room". In these rooms, four bookshelves, two each in the bedroom and the living room, stood out. The bookshelves in the living room were full of books on China, its literature, history and philosophy, in addition to books on TCM, and included ancient classics, such as *The Collected Works of Pre-Qin Philosophers* and *The Four Books and Five Classics*[2], and works by 20th century writers, including *Dawn Blossoms Plucked at Dusk* and *A Brief Introduction to the History of Chinese Literature*.

Jean enjoyed talking with his Chinese friends, 'chit-chatting', he called it. His conversations aided his studies. His research on the provincial officials and the civil service system of the Ming dynasty, TCM, and the ancient Chinese culture, largely resulted from such 'chit-chat'. Even when he had difficulty getting about in his later years, Jean still liked discussing Chinese history and culture with his friends. When a fact or literary quotation slipped his mind, he would point at a book on the shelf and ask a friend to hand it to him. These dazzling books on China in history and modern times reflected the heartfelt love of a French Sinologist for the Chinese culture.

In reality, his embrace of Chinese culture was a gradual process. Jean once told his friends his feelings for Chinese culture grew from an initial interest, to love, and finally, to worship. He once told friends that were gathered around him, that he worshiped the Chinese culture. For a western scholar, we can guess his profound passion, when he applied the wording 'worship'. It was an affirmation of the effect of Chinese culture on his life and his soul.

Among the sages in ancient China, Jean favoured Lao Tzu, a philosopher in the Spring and Autumn period, and the founder of Taoism. On Jean's bookshelf there were four versions of *Tao Te Ching*, translated into French. Among them, a version translated from German into French was

---

[2] Four Books: **The Great Learning, The Doctrine of the Mean, The Confucian Analects**, and **The Works of Mencius**; Five Classics: **The Book of Songs, The Book of History, The Book of Changes, The Book of Rites** and **The Spring and Autumn Annals**.

his favourite. He had a copy of it duplicated specially, and asked Yang Chenguang to give it to Professor Léon Vandermeersch, his friend at the French National Centre for Scientific Research, when Yang went to France. One year, Jean prepared to partner with Su Xinghua, to translate *Tao Te Ching*. Su Xinghua translated it from classical Chinese into the vernacular, which was then translated into French by Jean. For various reasons, the translation was not finished. Although only one chapter was translated, Jean's prudence and care deeply impressed Su Xinghua: "When we discussed *Tao Te Ching*, we spent 20 hours in one week, just discussing the first chapter. His dedication for knowledge really 'shocked' me, at 25. It effected my academic attitude in the future."

One of Jean's bookshelves

In Jean's mind, whereas Confucianism stresses the distinction between the noble and the humble and the hierarchical order, Taoism, represented by Lao Tzu, was the real base of Chinese culture. If one traces things carefully back to their source, the earliest people-based thought in Chinese culture was not the idea that "the people are more important than the monarch" advocated by Mencius but the source can be traced back to Lao Tzu. In *Tao Te Ching*, Jean often quoted: "The saints should decide their will according to the will of the ordinary people." Considering the kindness of Jean in his daily life, it is easy to understand why he showed such esteem for Lao Tzu. In truth, the influence of Taoism on Jean cannot be fully expressed by this one sentence. *Tao Te Ching* clearly proposes, in Chapter 2 that: "The saints let things take their own course and teach others, not by words but by deeds." Although he never regarded himself as a saint, and refused to be labelled with the quality of sublimity, his words and deeds reflected his adherence to 'teaching others, not by words but by deeds'. Those familiar with Jean know that he never directly criticised others, or promoted his beliefs in a big way. He proceeded with everyday matters and influenced and helped others around him, by his words and deeds. A Chinese saying observes: "A man of true worth attracts admiration." Jean handled affairs in a profound, restrained manner, and influenced numerous people.

Some of the many books collected by Jean

Chapter 2

In addition to Lao Tzu, Jean also highly praised Wang Yangming, a philosopher of the Ming dynasty. As with Lao Tzu, Jean's acceptance of Wang Yangming did not merely rest in philosophy. Jean discovered the universal pursuit of mankind for the conscience, through Wang Yangming. He once said: "Conscience is the best gift to mankind bestowed by God." The tenet of the 'philosophy of mind' is to 'attain conscience': "Those who have conscience are saints. The essence of the saint is to attain conscience." It can be said that Jean discovered the similarities of eastern and western cultures' values through Wang Yangming.

To help the western world to know more about traditional Chinese culture, Jean cooperated with his French friends, including Léon Vandermeersch, writing works such as *The Wisdom of China – Another Sort of Culture* and *The Wisdom of China*. In the preface of *The Wisdom of China*, Jean complimented Chinese culture: "The Chinese culture is the oldest culture among today's dynamic cultures. She boasts a history of more than 5,000 years and can be dated back to the pre historic period. Even if we regard the invention of the Chinese characters as the beginning of the Chinese culture, there is a history of 3,500 years… The Chinese culture blends ancient and modern times and boasts the longest history." He also wrote: "The achievements of the Greek thinking arose after the Renaissance… The Chinese thinking has probably not come to its end." Zhang Chi who taught in Northwest University, clearly remembers when Jean wrote *The Wisdom of China*. As Zhang Chi majored in Chinese language and literature as an undergraduate, Jean invited him to explain the structure of Chinese characters and the logic of word formation. In particular, Zhang Chi explained the 'phonogram' of the 'six categories of Chinese characters', because more than 80% of the Chinese characters were invented on that principle. Through the character pattern, the pronunciations and meanings of most characters can be judged, and new ones can be created to refer to new things, just like chemical elements. Zhang Chi illustrated the word formation with the Chinese character '化'. This character has a meaning in modern Chinese equivalent to the French and British English suffix '-isation', and the American English suffix '-ization'. Using it, infinite new derivative words of Chinese characters can be formed using basic words to express new ideas, for instance, 'modernisation', 'automation' and 'mechanisation'. Jean was thrilled with Zhang Chi's explanation and said that many western Sinologists thought Chinese words were formed without any logic or system, and believed that Chinese was the most difficult language to learn, when, in fact, it was that they did not know the logical method of word formation. Jean included Zhang Chi's views and example illustrations in his book. Afterwards, whenever his French friends visited him, he would invite Zhang Chi to explain to them the logic of formation of Chinese words, to arouse their interest in Chinese. He hoped that more westerners could reject the idea that 'Chinese characters are difficult to write and Chinese is difficult to learn' so that they could learn and know the Chinese history and culture.

Chapter 3
Building Sino-French Exchanges

A Parisian in Xi'an

Chapter 3

Historically, China and France have kept close cultural exchanges. The noted Silk Road extended from the city of Chang'an to Lyon in France. In the 18th century, French Enlightenment thinkers, like Voltaire and Denis Diderot, became very interested in Chinese culture, related in tales by missionaries returning from China. They wrote that China was a prosperous country, governed by an enlightened emperor, and seemed a paradise on earth, housing people living in peace and contentment. In the 1960s, China and France took the lead in establishing ambassadorial-level diplomatic relations. Jean undoubtedly fueled the long-term, Sino-French friendship.

1. A Willing Envoy of Sino-French Cultural Exchanges

As a French man profoundly interested in the Chinese culture, Jean began to expedite Sino-French cultural exchanges of his own accord. It can be said that, in one sense, Jean attached more importance to his role as an envoy of Sino-French exchanges than as a French expert in culture and education. Whenever his French friends came to China, however many there were, he would invite his Chinese friends, including Lu Dong of XISU, to have an informal discussion with them and teach them traditional Chinese culture. Often, during the lecture, the Chinese friends lectured to them in Chinese, and Jean interpreted. Jean often told his French friends travelling in China: "It's not enough to simply visit the scenic spots in China. What's more important is to understand the Chinese culture and people." Jean acted as a guide, and took his French friends to visit Xi'an. The Greater Wild Goose Pagoda, Xingjiao temple, Louguantai, Forest of Steles and Dangjia village were all favourite destinations to take his French friends.

After retiring from XISU, Jean did not stop working to enjoy his twilight years, instead, despite his age and frailty, he devoted himself to researching the history of the Ming dynasty in China. It seemed perplexing to many people. One day, Jia Zhenfan of XISU asked Jean: "What on earth do you research so diligently for?" Jean replied: "To help the French to know more about the traditional Chinese culture." To avoid a cultural misunderstanding, Jean refused to introduce some terrifying details of the brutal corporal punishment applied in the royal court of the Ming dynasty to French readers. There may be different ideas why he did this, but Jean's consideration deserves our admiration, given the complexity of cross-cultural exchanges. When he introduced

Chinese culture to the French people, Jean also actively introduced the French culture to China. Many of his lectures to XISU teachers and students had themes of French history and culture. Jean also invited French Sinologists and writers to China, and introduced research on Sinology and Chinese literature in France, including the prestigious French Sinologist, Léon Vandermeersch, and the celebrated poet, Hugues de Montalembert.

Jean signing at the inaugural meeting of the Sino-French Science & Technology Exchanges Association, May 1998

In order that French friends, from all walks of life, could know China better, Jean repeatedly contacted and facilitated a French delegation to visit, so that more French people could know about Chinese history, culture, and its reform. For years, Jean had been on good terms with the French embassy in China, and French ambassadors visited Xi'an many times. In May 2014, Madame Sylvie Bermann paid a special visit to Jean, and affirmed his lifelong dedication to education and his achievements.

In the mid-1980s, to nurture good Sino-French relations at a higher level, Jean tried to help Xi'an and Lyon to become sister cities. The two cities, one in the eastern hemisphere, the other in the western hemisphere, were at the start and end of the Silk Road. Jean's efforts to establish the relationship between the two cities showed courage and far-sightedness. Sadly, however, his endeavours failed.

Chapter 3

In Jean's mind, scientific-technical exchanges should be placed above cultural exchanges. Jean's initial idea was to facilitate Sino-French, scientific-technical exchanges, which would drive bi-lateral cultural exchanges. As a result, Jean did all he could to enhance Sino-French scientific-technical exchanges. To fuel collaboration and exchanges in the 1990s, Jean proposed and supported, an initiative by Geng Qingyi, the former deputy director-general of Shaanxi Province Health Department, Yi Guilu, deputy chief of Xi'an Sanitation and Anti-epidemic Station and Hu Sishe, a young XISU scholar, studying in France, and others, to build the Sino-French Science & Technology Exchanges Association. The inauguration was in May 1998, and attended by Chen Zongxing, former vice governor of Shaanxi province and Pierre Morel, former French ambassador in China. At the meeting, Zhou Lian, director of the North-West Institute

Jean and his friends in Xi'an, in the summer of 2000

Jean, accompanying Geng Qingyi (right) of the Shaanxi Province Health Department, visiting the office of AIDS experts at the Institut Pasteur in Paris, France, October 1997

for Non-ferrous Metal Research, who had studied in France, was elected as its first president. Dr Hu Sishe was appointed secretary general and Jean was the adviser. The Association's office was in the XSIU hotel. The aim of the Association was to establish long-term, Sino-French governmental exchanges and to subsidise more Chinese students to study in France. Although it did not last long, the Association helped a group of young Chinese from the scientific and technological, and cultural circles, to study in France, and pushed Sino-French collaboration and exchanges.

Francois Preshion French ambassador in China, conferring the Legion d'Honneur on Jean, on behalf of the French government, 6 May 1994

Pierre Morel, then the French ambassador in China, presenting Jean with a scroll reading '友谊' ('friendship') in Xi'an, to celebrate Jean's 80th birthday, August 1999

Chapter 3

Francois Liu (second from right), vice president of the Sino-French Science & Technology Exchanges Association, delivering a speech at the inaugural meeting of the Association, May 1998

Celebrating the 20th anniversary of Jean's teaching at XISU, November 1996

During his 40 years in Xi'an, Jean made great efforts to accelerate Sino-French cultural exchanges, and to strengthen the friendship of the two countries. Using his contacts with all social sectors in France, he positively stimulated and helped his Chinese friends to study and to conduct cultural exchanges in France, while introducing many French friends to cultural exchanges and giving lectures in China. To commend Jean's outstanding contributions to Sino-French cultural exchanges, Francois Preshion, French ambassador in China, travelled to Xi'an on 5 May, 1994, and conferred the National Order of the Legion of Honour (Legion d'Honneur) on Jean, on behalf of the French president. The Legion d'Honneur is the highest order of merit awarded in France. After being granted the honour, Jean immediately made it a present to XISU for its permanent collection. As Jean said, he won the honour because of his friendship and cooperation with the Chinese people and should share it with them. May the Sino-French cultural exchanges last forever, just like the medal received in China. At the award ceremony, Jean made an affectionate speech:

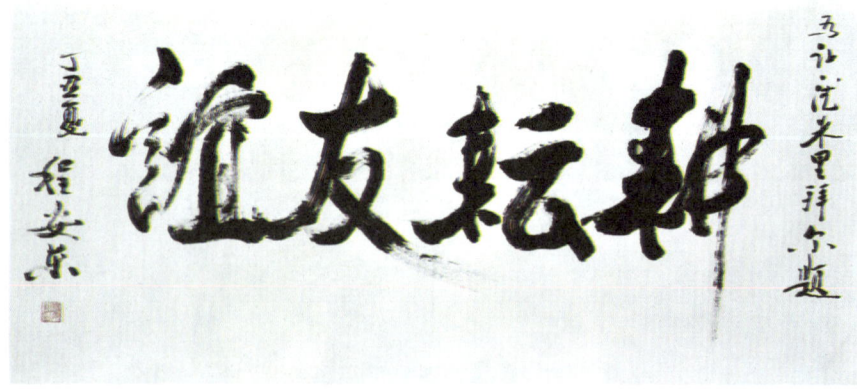

Then-governor of Shaanxi province, Cheng Andong's autograph, '耕耘友谊' (meaning 'cultivating friendship'), in honour of Jean, 1997

"Xi'an used to be a well-known city boasting a population of one million, even in the Tang dynasty, and was also the largest city in the world then. Caravans came there in an endless stream from the west, carrying valuable gifts for the emperors.

"Today, Your Excellency Ambassador, your arrival has continued that tradition. You brought a gift to me, a medal, which functions as a token.

Chapter 3

Jean at Dr. Wu Hua's art exhibition in Paris in 1993

Jean and his friend, Léon Vandermeersch, a French Academy of Sciences, Sinologist, in Xi'an, 10 December 2006

Guy Blaudin de Thé a French academic visiting Jean in Xi'an in August 2010

Jean and Francois Hominal, president of the Ricci Institute, France, in Xi'an in 2011

"The wings of the medal, pointing east and west, call for the east and the west to draw close. It stimulates the integration of the fine quality and good talents of the Chinese and French people, and the extraordinary competence, unique endurance, everlasting patience, outstanding intelligence and marvellous capability of the Chinese people, with the rational thinking and generous minds of the French people.

"The wings of the medal, reaching out to the earth, also indicate to the special demands of human beings since the beginning of the century, and require each labourer to ceaselessly exploit and utilise the resources of the earth, for the benefit of mankind.

"The wings of the medal reaching out to the sky remind all of us to support the loftiest aspirations of mankind, to seek truth and justice, and practice benevolence, lenience and kindness.

"It reminds us that all the great achievements of mankind have been made with blood, the most valuable gift of the mankind.

"Meanwhile, it pays tributes to the Chinese, the French people and others around the world, who save others, at the expense of their own lives.

"Mr. Ambassador, you conferred on me the medal, on behalf of the French people, and I'll present it to the representative of the Chinese people, to preserve it, to show my greatest respect and appreciation for the Chinese people. I have sensed the courage of the Chinese farmers and workers, the alertness and resourcefulness of the Chinese technical experts, the capability of the Chinese scientists and writers, the selflessness of the Chinese medical staff, the competence of the Chinese administrative staff, the talent of the Chinese artists and the glamour of the Chinese poets.

"In the meantime, I'd like to convey my gratitude to Chinese people, those present and elsewhere, who have given me enthusiastic, persistent help and cordial and sincere friendship.

"In closing, I'll hand it over to the Chinese people to preserve it to show my friendship to you!"

2. Efforts to Subsidise Chinese Students in France

When he began to teach French in XISU, Jean noticed the students' thirst for knowledge of, and interest in, the outside world. At the time, the Cultural Revolution had just come to an end, and while many things needed to be done, the closed environment meant that young people were impatient to see the outside world. Nevertheless, it was not possible to go abroad then. For this reason, Jean, in his sixties, bravely assumed the responsibility and did his utmost to help these young people, eager to 'open their eyes to see the world'.

Jean made good use of his various relations in France to create more opportunities for young people to study abroad. The XISU teachers and students were lucky to become the first recipients of Jean's help. Soon, young, overseas Chinese students, studying in France, assisted with a subsidy from Jean, came from far and wide, bringing talents such as foreign languages, economics, medicine, geology, mass media, science and technology, literature, art and business. Despite their different walks of life, they shared common traits, namely, diligence and a poor family background. As a result, Jean used his own money to subsidise these poor students. Years later, the students returning from studying overseas said that it would have been impossible for them to study abroad without Jean. Li Tao, general manager of Shaanxi Huasheng (Group), was one of the first students subsidised by Jean to go abroad. He recalled the difficulty adjusting to the environment, the moment he arrived in France. At that time, Li Tao, a correspondent of Xi'an Television, could live a decent life with his monthly salary of Rmb50 at home, but the subway fare of 12 francs, and travelling expenses over two days, used up his month's salary. Jean provided Li Tao with funds for his study and living expenses, from his own savings and arranged for Li Tao to live in the house of one of his French friends who provided his accommodation free of charge. Numerous other students were subsidised by Jean to study in France.

Jean's finances were limited, however. In order to help these students, Jean applied to the French government and relevant departments for more scholarships. The students enjoying French government scholarships could receive special care, and the French International Student Centre provided insurance and housing for the students and organised for them to travel in France. The favourable conditions for learning and living would have been impossible without Jean's arduous efforts.

French Sinologist Léon Vandermeersch came to Xi'an on 10 December 2006, and met XISU students in Jean's home

Chapter 3

Jean, Li Tao, Chen Lei, Chen Jun and Su Chao, receiving a delegation of the 'Fourth World', headed by Bai Yajian and Yang Shuxiu, in Xi'an in 2006

Professor Guy Blaudin de Thé (left), an academic of French Academy of Sciences, celebrating Jean's birthday in Xi'an, August 2010

With the help of Jean, many doctors in Xi'an, especially some TCM doctors, got the chance to study for a degree or to do scientific research and cultural exchanges in France. Why was Jean interested in helping the doctors? Many years later, in an interview with *Xi'an Evening News*, he said: "Doctors can save people's lives, and helping a doctor means helping numerous people." His benevolence is worthy of our admiration. Jean also held the view that: "Westerners are not familiar with TCM. The Chinese doctors studying abroad can learn advanced modern medicine and, at the same time, take the essence of TCM abroad and progress it. The combination of the western medicine and the TCM will be an amazing accomplishment."

As one of the first experts for Sino-French exchanges, Jean came to teach in XISU at the age of 57 and retired at 65. During those eight years, he helped groups of Chinese overseas students in France. Even after his retirement, he still enjoyed doing this, whatever the subjects for study or exchanges. Jean said he did that only to help more French people to know and understand the Chinese culture, and more Chinese people to study abroad, and then return to 'serve the Chinese people'. Jean had only one requirement for those who studied in France with his help: to return to China and serve their country.

3. Meticulous Care for Overseas Chinese Students in France

Jean came to China when he was almost 60 years old and troubled by illness. However, in order to help the Chinese students, he made unimaginable effort. After retiring, and before becoming a 'permanent foreign resident' in Shaanxi, he had to return to France to apply for a visa each year. This was a difficult journey for the elderly, ill Jean. Nonetheless, he turned these difficulties into favourable conditions and made them positive, to help the students to study in France make contact with the universities and apply for scholarships. Jean suffered from severe hyper-tension and colitis, and had undergone 13 operations, yet he still persisted in helping every young person who came to him, despite struggles against pain, and he never tired or gave up on his beliefs due to pain. Jean frequently used a gesture — holding up a fist, and shouting loudly: "Fighting! Fighting!" He won opportunities for the students of China, especially Xi'an, to study in France and the scholarships from France relied on his struggling, unyielding spirit. His struggling spirit

Chapter 3

definitely influenced each Chinese overseas student in France. Once, Ling Ming and Zhu Weimin, orthopedists subsidised by Jean, came to France several days after Jean had undergone an operation in Paris. Regardless of his recuperation after a major illness, Jean personally sent Ling Ming to Lyon and Zhu Weimin to Marseilles. He not only explained the issues for the overseas studies of the two doctors, but also brought Zhu Weimin to go through the formalities. Noticing Jean clutching his wound, Zhu Weimin felt exceedingly sad and persuaded Jean: "I can handle these matters myself later. We are not going together, OK?" But Jean replied: "It doesn't matter. I should do whatever I can to help you, my children." After repeated persuasion from Zhu Weimin, Jean agreed to return to Paris to rest, but he still felt anxious about leaving, and handed over some of Zhu Weimin's unsettled problems to a friend in Marseilles, to handle.

Prunus cerasifera blooming outside the foreign faculty residence

Jean's help for the Chinese overseas students in France did not end with their arrival in France. It was just the beginning. During a return visit to his family in France, he would bring with him a wealth of data about the Chinese students every day, for future studies in France. If the Chinese students had just arrived in France and Jean happened to be there, he would meet the young student in person. The first stop for the Chinese students was Jean's dormitory in the 13th arrondissement (Chinese quarter) in Paris. The newcomers could see many familiar-looking faces when they stepped into the door. It seemed to be the 'supreme headquarters' of the newly arrived Chinese students in France. Jean provided free accommodation to the overseas students in France, and stayed in the house of his relatives or friends. In addition, Jean also mobilised his relatives and friends to care for and look after the Chinese students in France. During the study overseas of Zhu Weimin and Ling Ming in either Marseilles or Lyon, Jean's friends often called on them and asked whether they encountered any difficulties in life and work, and drove them to their home to celebrate festivals or to have meals. Thanks to Jean's meticulous care, the Chinese students spent the period of learning and internship without difficulties or loneliness in France. Jean helped so many overseas students that greeting cards from all corners of the world flooded the small house in the foreign faculty residence of XISU on the occasion of his birthday every year.

4. An Inspiration to Chinese Students in France

'Maybe' always prefaced Jean's utterances. To the Chinese students who came to him, Jean often replied: "Maybe I can help you." He never bragged, but tried his utmost, without any evasion or upset. Jean successively subsidised up to 50 talented students for their study and cultural exchanges in France, most of whom returned to China after their studies and made contributions in their own specialty areas, industries or fields. Wang Liqun, then chief physician of the department of orthopaedics of Shaanxi Friendship Hospital, was representative of them. Today, Wang Linqun, is in his sixties, and has been to Malawi, Africa three times, as one of the doctors providing assistance in the construction of Africa. The medical environment in Africa was perilous as it was an area with a high-prevalence of AIDS. Any carelessness in surgical operations would bring the danger of being infected. Wang Liqun proceeded without any hesitation and persisted in fighting on the front line of the efforts to help Africa, influenced by Jean's spirit of selfless devotion. In recollecting Jean, Wang Liqun said: "Mr. Jean de Miribel changed my life and my personality. It is a blessing for me to have known him. I should repay his kindness by amplifying his benevolence in my future work and life. I will help more patients with my love and skills, in return for my dearest motherland, where I was born, grew up and nurtured, and for the cultivation of me by Jean and France." Indeed, Jean's help to the Chinese students in France not merely influenced their lives and studies but also their minds. Whenever he encountered difficulties during his studies in France, Wang Liqun often thought of what Jean usually said: "That's life" ("ça, c'est la vie"), and felt relieved.

Chapter 3

Jean in his study

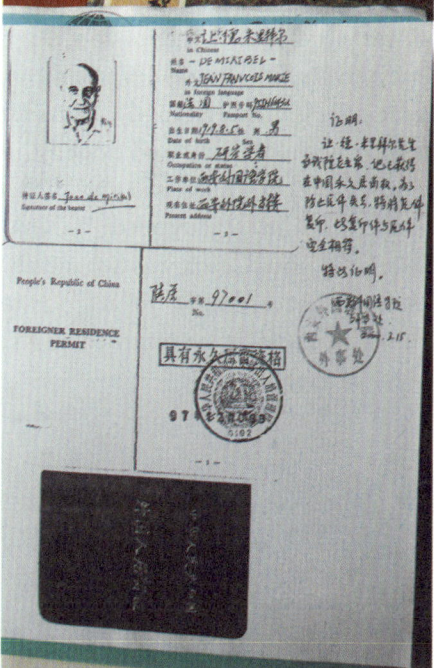
A copy of Jean's permanent residency permit

5. "My roots are in Xi'an"

Jean retired in July 1984. However, he was reluctant to leave China and applied to the Chinese Ministry of Education for leave to stay, in February 1984. The Ministry of Education replied in May and invited Jean to continue to live in China until the end of the year in gratitude for his support for China's educational course and his positive contributions to enhancing Sino-French relations. His future demands were to be discussed with XISU. Jean lived in China until his death. To continue to live in China, a feeble Jean took the trouble to return to France each year, in the capacity of a research scholar, to apply for a work visa. To facilitate Jean's life and work in China, XISU invited him to be the guest researcher of the Office of Comparative Research on Chinese and French Culture in 1985, and granted him the title of lifelong, honourary professor in 1995.

Former Secretary, Sun Lijian, of the German department at XISU, worked in the Chinese embassy in France from 1994 to 1996. Once, Jean made a special trip to meet Sun when he was applying for the visa in France. They talked in Chinese in a French street and the French passers-by were greatly surprised to see a French man speak fluent Chinese in a

French street. Sun Zhijian felt distressed that the 70-year-old man shuttled between the two countries applying for visas and asked why he did not return to live in France. Jean replied: "I'm only a passer-by in France. My home is in China." Actually, Jean's mother, who lived in France had been missing her eldest son and hoped that he could return. His mother once said in a letter: "I need you and the family needs you," but Jean had made his life in China. He replied: "China needs me more and my roots are in Xi'an." To Jean, China was not merely his second home, but his permanent residence. Accordingly, he set out to apply for permanent residence in China the moment he returned to Xi'an.

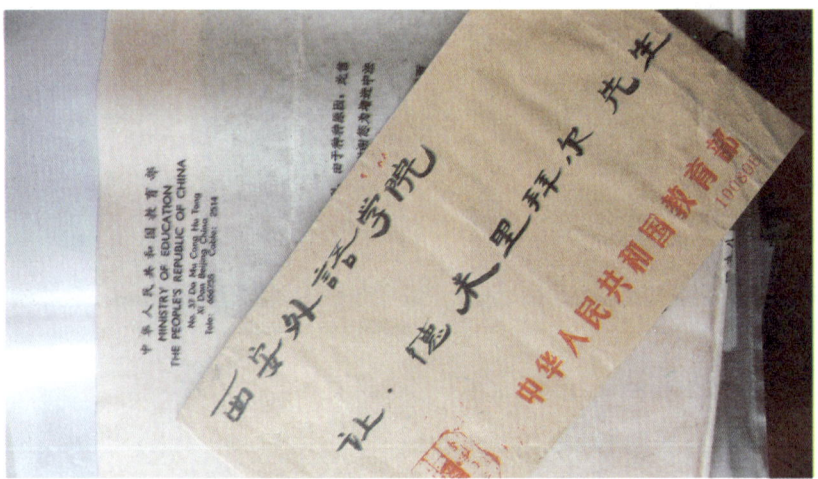

Ministry of Education's reply to Jean in 1984

With the special approval of then-Provincial Governor, Cheng Andong, Jean got the permanent residency permit as a 'research scholar' on 18 June, 1997, and became the first foreign expert qualified for permanent residence in China in Xi'an, and in the whole Shaanxi province since the founding of the People's Republic of China. On the day the permit was issued, Jean wore his only formal dress to attend the ceremony. Taking his hard-won permanent residence permit from the official at the Foreign Affairs Office of the People's Government of Shaanix Province, Jean made a deep bow and was filled with gratitude. At the permit issuing ceremony, Jean spoke with emotion: "Today, I'd like to convey my thanks to all the people who helped me become a permanent foreign resident in China. On 18 June 1940, General de Gaulle called on the French people in London to resist and give France hope. I really appreciate you choosing this date to grant me the permanent residence permit, which symbolises the permanent friendship between the Chinese and French people!"

Chapter 3

中华人民共和国教育部
MINISTRY OF EDUCATION
THE PEOPLE'S REPUBLIC OF CHINA
No. 37 Da Mu Cang Hu Tong
Xi Dan Beijing China
Tele: 666758　Cable: 2514

德·米里拜尔先生：

　　您二月十七日给何东昌部长的信已经收到。由于种种原因，此信迟复为歉。我们要谢谢您对我国的教育事业的支持，谢谢您为增进中法两国人民之间的友谊所作的积极贡献。

　　您希望在合同期满后能再客居西安外语学院两年。最近我听说西外在您今年七月结束教学后，为了答谢您的出色工作和友谊，准备挽留您居住到八四年底。如您尚有其它要求，我建议您与该院具体协商。

　　祝愿您

工作顺利、身体健康！

教育部外事局专家处处长

一九八四年五月二十四日

Ministry of Education's reply to Jean in 1984

A Parisian in Xi'an

Jean and Wang Bin in front of the Beijing Hotel in 1980

Chapter 3

Pierre Morel, then French ambassador in China, came especially to Xi'an to celebrate Jean's 80th birthday on 5 August 1999 and wrote two big Chinese characters '友谊' (meaning 'friendship') with a writing brush, as his gift to Jean. This affirmed and commended Jean's years of effort to promote the friendship between China and France and between the two peoples.

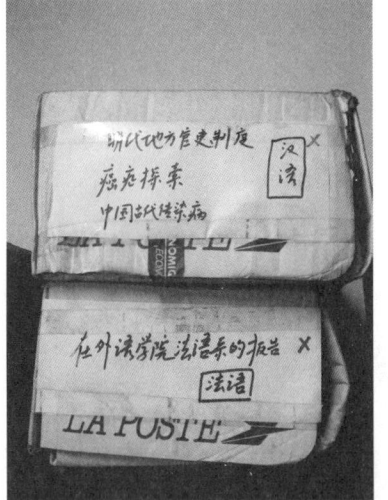

In 1997, then Governor of Shaanxi province, Cheng Andong autographed '耕耘友谊' (meaning 'cultivating friendship') which has been engraved in the monument for Jean on the Yanta campus of XISU. More importantly, it has been engraved in the minds of all of Jean's Chinese friends!

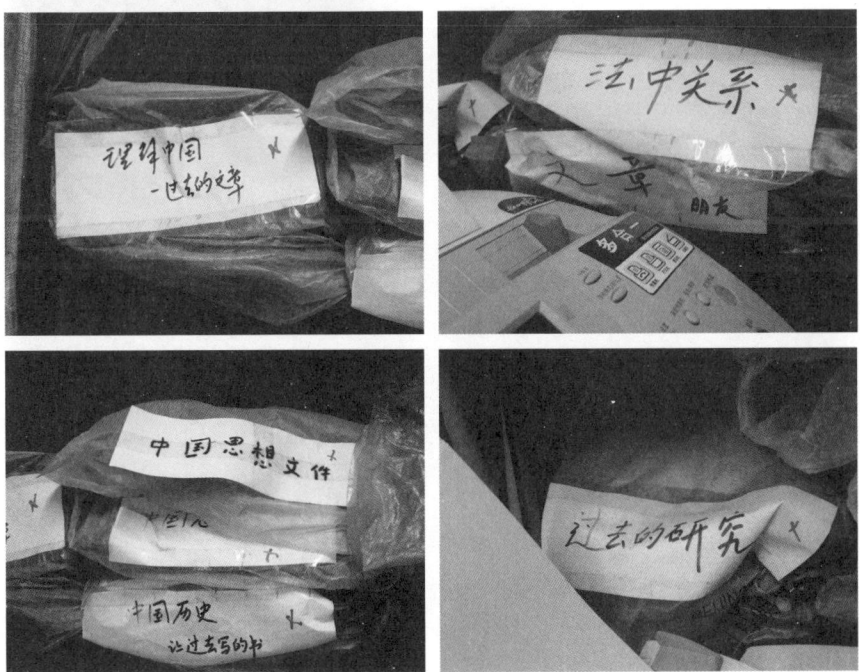

Jean's research data

Chapter 4

Friendship with the Chinese People

After retirement, Jean busied himself studying Chinese culture and rode his bicycle around the streets to be among the grass roots community in Xi'an, and the whole Shaanxi province, to know their living conditions and try his best to help them. His benevolence benefited many people. As a result, he made many friends with many citizens in Xi'an, including leaders at the provincial and department levels, the elite in the scientific and technological circles, medical circles, mass media, and more ordinary workers in the society. It can be said that Jean made friends all over the ancient city during 40 years of living in Xi'an.

Jean in his study

Jean surrounded himself with Chinese culture

1. Adept at Making Friends

Jean was good at making friends. Born into a noble French family, with many connections, Jean himself had many friends, most of whom were authorities in their field, for instance, Professor Léon Vandermeersch, research director of the Paris (French) Institute of Advanced Study, Hugues de Montalembert, a prestigious poet, Michel Grolleaud, a UN agricultural expert, Pierre Rainero, a French astrophysicist and educator, Guy Blaudin de Thé, a French academic of medical biology, Francois Cheng, an academic of French literature, and his daughter, Anne Cheng, an expert of Sinology. It was with the generous backing of his friends that Jean could help groups of Chinese students to study in France and assist with their learning and living. Jean travelled in more than 70 countries in the first half of his life and he made many international friends all over the world. On his bookshelves were the autographed works of many famous scholars, collected by Jean. Whatever nationality they were, they made friends with Jean through admiration for his selfless dedication, boundless love and charming personality. However, more of Jean's friends lived in the ancient city of Xi'an.

Jean, Geng Qiang (left) and Jean's little brother, at the Qian mausoleum, 1999

Jean, Yin Baoku (first from right), Zhang Cheng (third from right), Chen Lei (second from left) and Su Chao (left), touring Xingjiao temple, 2002

The first friends Jean made in China were the teachers and students of XISU, because of his work and teaching. They included Lu Dong, former library curator of XISU and former vice chairman of Shaanxi provincial committee of the Chinese People's Political Consultative Conference (CPPCC), Guo Taichu, French education expert, translator and professor of XISU, Hu Sishe, former president of XISU, member of the standing committee of the KMT central committee and vice chairman of the Chinese People's Association for Friendship with Foreign Countries, Liang Jialin, librarian, compiler, reviewer of XISU, deputy director of literary translation committee of Shaanxi Translation Association and director of Xi'an Welfare Foundation for the Disabled, Wang Kejian, former first director of the department of German, French and Spanish of XISU and former director of Shaanxi Province Tourism Bureau, Ren Zhanfeng, former party secretary of the department of French and Spanish of XISU and former vice president of the labour union of XISU, Jia Zhenfan, teacher of XISU, Zhang Xiaohui and Yang Jingbo, founders and technical directors of Xi'an Shiwen Software Co., Ltd. Their friendships began when Jean taught in XISU. With the introduction of these friends, Jean's contacts expanded in China. In this way, Jean made friends with Geng Qingyi, then deputy director of Shaanxi Province Health Department, master supervisor of Chinese Academy of Preventive Medicine, part-time professor of Xi'an Jiaotong University Health Science Centre, Yang Chenguang, deputy director of the oncology department of Shaanxi Province Hospital of Traditional Chinese Medicine, Li Tao, general manager and vice president of Shaanxi Huasheng (Group) Corp., Qu Lijun, researcher of Moral Research Centre of Shaanxi History Museum and Wang Liqun,

Jean, Duan Xianglong and his wife, Li Fang (second from right) and Wang Heng (right), 1 January, 2002

Jean, Wang Xiaoying and Zhang Bin, in the Peach Garden in the northern suburbs of Xi'an, 23 March, 2003

chief physician of the department of orthopaedics of Shaanxi Friendship Hospital. Jean subsidised many young students with great potential, and changed the course of their lives.

Jean's friends included not only teachers at universities, intellectuals, medical experts, members of the elite, government officials and important people, but also a myriad of grass roots labourers. What an amazing range of contacts for Jean! The worldly distinction of people was meaningless to him. In his view, they had only one identity - his friends. He showed most concern about his grass roots, poor friends in need. He often said: "I like ordinary people." He made friends with a policeman in an unusual way. It was not long after he had come to China, when the teachers of the department of German, French and Spanish, knowing that Jean liked Chinese culture, took him to visit the Giant Buddhist temple in Binxian county. At that time the Cultural Revolution had just come to an end and many places had not been opened to foreigners. Jean's visit, without prior approval, attracted the attention of the department concerned. The public security organisation asked him to answer some questions, including the purpose of his visit to Binxian county. Jean insisted that he was there just to make an on-the-spot investigation out of admiration for the Chinese history and culture. But the policeman did not completely believe his simple response, and continued to question him. Finally, Jean had to mention his family background: "My cousin was a confidential secretary of President Charles de Gaulle and I'm friendly to the Chinese people." Although he had arrived in China not long before, wise Jean had mastered the social protocol of the country, and he knew that this trump card could help him at the critical moment. His answer astonished the policeman. In the situation of the Cold War in 1964, the Western capitalist countries did not accept the People's Republic of China and isolated China politically, blocked China economically and threatened China militarily. Nevertheless, with his extraordinary strategic vision, French President Charles de Gaulle resolutely made a historic decision to establish full diplomatic relations with the People's Republic of China, which opened the door to mutual understanding and exchanges between China and France, and, at the same time, between China and the western world. Consequently, thanks to the influence of the former French President, who had facilitated the establishment of Sino-French diplomatic relations, Jean won the trust of the public security organisation. Unexpectedly, the policeman questioning him became a friend, and visited Jean years later with a pair of leather shoes as a gift. Jean valued the shoes and wore them for many years.

Jean, Sun Zhenjiao (left) and Huang Yingnian (right) touring Shanghai Oriental Pearl TV Tower in 2003

A Parisian in Xi'an

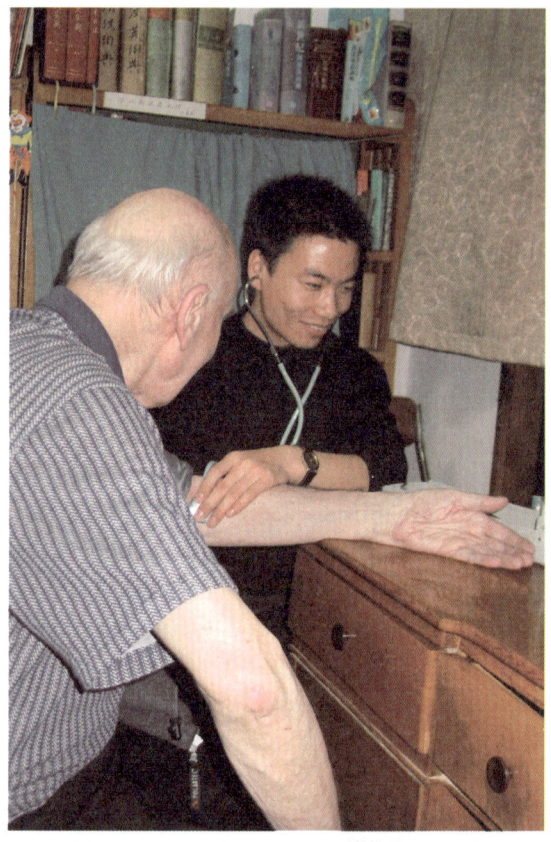

Doctor Yin Baoku with Jean in 2004

Jean and his friend talking to a vagrant in the Wolong temple, Xi'an

Chapter 4

Jean, Hu Sishe (left), former president of XISU and present vice chairman of the Chinese People's Association for Friendship with Foreign Countries, and Geng Qingyi, former deputy director of Shaanxi Province Health Department

Children wishing Jean good health and long life for his 85th birthday, 5 August, 2005

2. Helping Others to Fulfill Their Dreams

Jean had made numerous friends and was always ready to help others fulfill their dreams, which demonstrated Jean's reverence for the traditional virtues of China. Zhao Chengxun, who used to translate for Jean, was deeply impressed on that point. After the reform and opening up, the Shiyan (Hubei) Second Automobile Factory and French Citroen International began a cooperation project and Zhao Chengxun was invited to offer French training to their workers. To facilitate teaching, Zhao Chengxun compiled a textbook, *Introduction to French*[1] based on automobile manufacturing. Jean took the time to proofread the whole book for Zhao Chengxun, and wrote the preface for it.

Jean had an instant camera, which was rarely seen in China in the 1980s and 1990s; most people did not have the chance to ever see one. Film was very expensive and difficult to buy. Nevertheless, Jean generously lent it to his Chinese friends. Then, Zhao Chengxun's family lived in a rural area. Jean considerately lent his camera and film to Zhao Chengxun and asked him to take pictures of his family members and show him the photos. Jean intended to help the family of his friend, Zhao Chengxun, and ease the pain of him missing his family. Cui Shengrui, a cook at XISU Foreign Affairs Service Centre, made the acquaintance of Jean during a visit to a conference at Yangjialing, organised by the university in the winter of 1973. At that time, Cui simply felt the foreigner spoke Chinese fairly well. Unexpectedly, after a short meeting, Jean's approachability deeply touched Cui, who became a bosom friend of Jean. Cui's child fell and was hurt on his third birthday, in 1982. In order to cheer him up on his birthday, Jean took a photo of the child with the instant camera. It was an unforgettable incident to Cui.

Xing Zhiqiang, a plumber, began work at XISU, in 1997 and heard the stories about Jean. A fan of literature, Xing often borrowed books from Liang Jialin, exchanged book reviews with him and learned more information about Jean. Everyone showered praise on Jean, and Xing yearned to meet him. Taking the opportunity of repairing home appliances and handling trivial matters for him, Xing met Jean. Suffering from bad digestion and stomach troubles, he and Jean shared common topics. Their talks ranged from diseases to livelihood, life and enthusiasm for reading,

---

[1] French title: *Manuel d'initiation au français*

and medicine. Jean often communicated with Xing in the Shaanxi dialect, which made Xing, accustomed to talking in the Shaanxi dialect, feel more welcome. Sincere and approachable, Jean was like a senior always caring for the juniors everywhere. Xing even felt that Jean treated him more cordially than his own parents. Even Xing's little brother, who had little contact with Jean, felt Jean's care more than his own parents. As he grew older, Jean became weaker in health. Even in the burning hot summer in Xi'an, Jean's poor health could not allow the use of the air-conditioning, nor could he even bear the wind from the fan at the lowest speed. He had no other choice but to endure the severe heat in a sweat. Xing was distressed for Jean's suffering and thought about refitting the fan. After repeated experiments, ingenious Xing made a regulator and installed it on the fan. Jean could finally enjoy a slow, clear breeze. Jean highly praised Xing and encouraged Xing, now in his forties, to try to make inventions, to research and continue his enthusiasm for invention rather than cover up his talent. After that, when Xing wanted to do some housework, like mopping or cleaning for Jean, Jean would take the tools from Xing's hand and told him seriously: "Don't do that. Your hands should be applied only to invention and research."

Geng Qiang, son of Geng Qingyi, was a correspondent of Shaanxi Television Station. Often hearing of Jean from his father, he could not help a sense of curiosity and reverence for the elderly man. For the sake of his career, he asked his father to introduce him to Jean, and planned to shoot a feature programme about Jean at the end of 1996. Nevertheless, modest Jean was not willing to attract the attention of others, and thought that what he had done was simple and ordinary, and there was nothing to boast about, let alone record or publicise. Jean advocated the ideology of the Taoism and was profoundly influenced by it. In 2012, Jean's friends wanted to publish an autograph album for him, but Jean waved 'no' again and again: "Thank you! But what I've done does not deserve your efforts to make it for me." As early as 1996, Jean declined Geng Qiang's request to film him, but did talk casually to him. In a congenial way, they chatted to their heart's content, like old friends. Just before noon, Jean asked Geng Qiang to have lunch in his house, and he cooked simple French fries. Without ostentation, Jean treated Geng Qiang, who had met him for the first time, as a confidant. Although the interview failed, Geng Qiang continued his friendship with Jean for more than 20 years, and became a sworn friend. The longer he knew

Jean, the more he admired Jean's acts of kindness and wanted to publicise his benevolence. An opportunity arose in October 2006, when a young correspondent, named Wei Jia, who just begun work in the TV station, wanted to gather news, and Geng Qiang recommended Jean to be his topic. As expected, Jean refused Geng Qiang's request for shooting. Nonetheless, fully prepared Geng Qiang told Jean: "Wei Jia has a secret crush on a girl at the TV station and can win her over if you agree to be interviewed. It is a chance for the chap to get close to his sweetheart, why don't you help him win her love?" Kind Jean was always ready to help others, and the Shaanxi audience saw the wise, lenient figure of the elderly man, his words and deeds on TV for the first time.

Geng Qiang, Li Gang and Jean's little brother getting together again in Xi'an, 2008

3. Cherished Priceless Friendship

Jean always treasured the gifts his friends gave him. The furnishings in Jean's house were simple and old-fashioned. In addition to two bookshelves, full of books, in the unadorned living room, was a conspicuous stand exhibiting gifts. All sorts of fancy goods with Chinese folk characteristics were placed on it, including miniature terracotta warriors, facial makeup, paper-cutting, calligraphy, paintings, China's cultural relics, photos of scenic spots, folk handiwork, and even pictures of children. They were all gifts from his students and friends and were treasured by him. He said: "I feel especially happy whenever I see these

Chapter 4

Jean and his friends in the house of France-based, Chinese pianist, Wang Bin (right) in Xi'an, August 2010

gifts every day." Jean cherished these gifts, not only because of their special characteristics of the Chinese culture, but also for the deep love of his students and friends for him.

Jean and his friends in August 2010

On the sofa in Jean's living hall was a cushion in the shape of a China doll. Jean's friend, pianist, Wang Bin, gave it to him as a gift so that he could rest comfortably on the sofa. Jean fixed it to the wall with Scotch tape and made it a decoration.

Jean, Liu Chao (left) and Xia Li (right) in the summer of 2010

Jean showed caring concern to Zhao Chengxun when he worked as Jean's translator. In return for Jean's care for him, Zhao's mother wanted to give Jean a gift. Zhao told his mother that Jean never accepted expensive gifts from his friends, but had eyes only for small, goodwill gifts. Zhao's mother thought of making, by hand, a pair of cloth shoes for Jean's mother in France. Jean appreciated the gift idea very much, and brought back his mother's shoe pattern when he returned from France during the summer holiday. Zhao's mother carefully sewed the shoe soles and uppers and made a pair of women's cloth shoes in the Chinese style (commonly known as 'strong cloth soles', a folk handicraft with special Chinese characteristics) for Jean's mother. Jean's mother was elated to receive the shoes and asked Jean to convey her gratitude to Zhao and Zhao's mother on her behalf. In 1979, Zhao Chengxun, whose family lived in a rural area, had a chance to work in Shaanxi Engineering College in Hanzhong, Shaanxi province, which could change the residence registration of his family, and enable the whole family to reunite. At that time, Zhao Chengxun was working as Jean's translator. He was conflicted, on one hand, he hated to leave Jean, yet, on the other, feared his specialty of French would be affected. Hearing about it, Jean did not hold Zhao Chengxun back, but encouraged him to work in Hanzhong. Jean told Zhao that

Children with garlands for Jean for his birthday, 5 August, 2012

Chapter 4

Jean in his living room at XISU

he should solve the family issue first because it was of more importance, and he would have other chances to work in French in the future. In the second year that Zhao Chengxun worked in Shaanxi Engineering College, Jean wrote to him and asked him to find Bi Shengmei, Jean's first translator in XISU and a teacher of the department of French of XISU. He wanted an UNDEWUNDE French typewriter, produced in Spain brought from France by Jean, to help Zhao's study and work. The shoe pattern of Jean's mother and the typewriter were cherished and preserved as the most valuable gifts, by Zhao Chengxun. Jean, like a friend and a mentor, paid for them entirely.

Jean did not marry, but he understood the Chinese attachment to family. Jean had treasured up many thick, worn-out address books, fastened with adhesive tape, recording the contact information (telephone numbers and email addresses) of his friends and their family members, including their parents, spouse and children. Jean often asked his friends for family photos. He wrote 'A souvenir for Professor Jean de Miribel, my most respected friend' on the back of the photo of Yang Zhen and Jia Lanfen, husband and wife, taken in the Xiaolangdi reservoir in 2006. The back of a group photo of Lu Dong and his wife Cheng Tianzhang taken in the tea hill of Shangluo in October 2007, reads: "Dear Jean, we miss you from time to time. Loving you. Lu Dong and Cheng Tianzhang". Group photos of many other friends, and their family members, with Jean were collected in his photo album.

Jean researching

Jean was always thankful to those who had helped him. One 1 January, Secretary Ren Zhanfeng, of the CPC general branch, and Director Zhang Ping, of the XISU French department, paid a visit to Jean on behalf of the department, and gave him a down jacket as a festival gift to keep out the cold. They thought that it was natural to give such a small gift to a foreign expert caring for XISU and making contributions to it all his life. Nevertheless, Jean looked exceedingly excited and expressed his thanks many times. He immediately put on the jacket, and showed it to Ren Zhanfeng and everyone present. Geng Qiang said he had learned quite a lot from Jean, especially, to say 'thank you' actively. For even trivial matters, Jean would always say: "Thank you for your kindness! Thanks a lot."

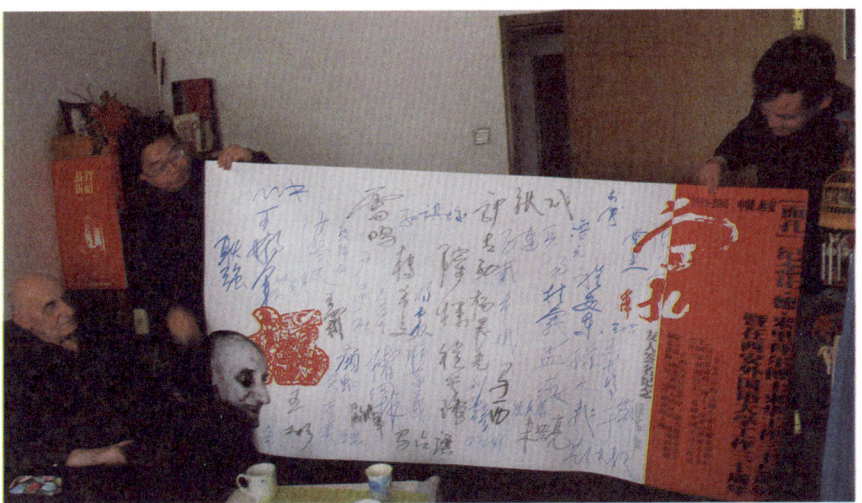
Jean treasured the poster carrying the signatures of his friends, in celebration of his birthday

4. Considerate to Others

Jean always took others to heart, and was considerate to others. Zhang Cheng, who had attended to Jean, said: "It is his habit to be thoughtful to others." On 23 November, 1996, the French department of XISU held a grand commemoration. A 'Celebration on the 20th Anniversary of Mr. Jean de Miribel's Teaching in French Department for 20 Years and the School Fellowship Party', took place in the Oriental Hotel. The department had invited Liang Jialin, yet although he promised to come, Liang still felt indecisive, due to his disability. Unexpectedly, before the party began, Jean abruptly appeared in Liang's office and solemnly, and personally, invited him to attend the celebration. Unexpectedly and extremely movingly, Jean took out a bill of Rmb50 and handed it over to Liang Jialin: "You have physical difficulties in attending. You can take a taxi then…" Greatly surprised, Liang immediately promised he would come. He refused Jean's money but Jean persisted until Liang said: "If you don't take back your money, I will not come. I mean it." Then Jean had to take back the money. Jean treated his friends sincerely and frankly without any hypocrisy.

Likewise, Jean always thought about others in trivial matters. For instance, Jean often received visitors at home in the foreign faculty residence where carpets were the first to be laid. To relieve the Chinese visitors of discomfort, Jean personally rolled up the carpet, made himself the same as others, and refused to enjoy any special treatment. For another example, an African teacher had come to teach in XISU and Jean asked Xing Zhiqiang to bring the 'little sun' (small solar heater) Jean used in winter for the African teacher, in case he should not be accustomed to the bitter cold winter in Xi'an. Another case was that, Jean did not like oatmeal, but Geng Qiang did not know this. Once, Geng Qiang cooked oatmeal for Jean, who did not raise any objection but ate it up happily. Geng Qiang also made French fries and used too much oil, and Jean suffered from indigestion the whole night. Jean repeatedly told Zhang Cheng, who took care of him that night, not to tell it to Geng Qiang for fear of making him feel guilty.

Gracious and hospitable in disposition, Jean liked his friends to come to his house very much. Whenever his friends visited him, he would always say: "Welcome! Make yourself at home, and feel at ease to do whatever you like." Jean fully trusted his friends. Some of his closest friends, such as Geng Qiang, Yang Chenguang and Li Tao, and his students, such as Xia Li, Liu Chao and Zhang Cheng, had the key to his door. Jean also left a key with the reception desk of the XISU Foreign Affairs Service Centre, so that his friends could come into his home more conveniently.

5. Paternal Love for His Students

Jean lived a single life and had no offspring, which often perplexed his Chinese friends. The majority could not accept the fact that a man in his seventies had lived a single life without any offspring. But it was quite different to Jean. He explained that he did not get married simply for fear that his love should shrink because of his family, and he could be benevolent to others without the bondage of marriage. Jean often called the Chinese students returning from overseas studies in France due to his subsidy, 'my children'. Indeed he had taken these young people as his own children. Once, Zhu Weimin paid a visit to Jean's home in China. Jean found that the sleeve of Zhu's clothes was ripped and took out his sewing kit to mend it. Zhu felt uneasy at having it mended by Jean, so he rushed to say: "I can do it myself." Jean did not permit it. They scrambled for the clothes but Jean won. Jean sewed Zhu's clothes and said smilingly: "You are a surgeon. You don't have the time. You are quite tired. It is a piece of cake for me. You are my child and I'm willing to do it for you." Zhu Weimin felt incredibly moved when he saw Jean assiduously wave his inexperienced big hands…

Chapter 4

Without a child of his own, Jean treated his students and young friends as if they were his own children. Despite thriftiness all his life, he generously helped the students. Not merely subsidising the Chinese students to study in France, he would also resolutely lend a helping hand when the families of domestic students encountered difficulties; helping their families with his meagre salary and subsidising them to go on learning. Over four decades, Jean helped numerous Chinese children from poverty-stricken families and subsidised more than 10 poor students of XISU to finish their college studies. In Jean's words, he aimed to "give everyone a fair opportunity to take off". In the autumn of 2009, Jean was admitted to Xi'an Friendship Hospital. Due to his illness, the hospital required him to stay in hospital for several days, for observation, but Jean insisted on leaving. He said: "Don't waste the money in hospital, but help more people to take off with it."

Jean's philanthropic, magnanimous acts were spread throughout XISU and moved numerous students. As Jean grew older, tradition had it that the students spontaneously came to take care of him, and the juniors would take their turn after the seniors graduated. It was almost groups of students that accompanied Jean while he was in Xi'an. Liu Chao, Xia Li and Zhang Cheng were their representatives. In comparison with their care for Jean, Jean offered them more care. The children cordially called him 'Grandpa Jean'. Liu Chao clearly remembered that, once he was on the way to buy vegetables for Grandpa Jean when it suddenly started to rain. When he came into the door, all wet, with a basket of vegetables in hand, Grandpa Jean prepared him a cup of warm red wine. What made Liu Chao shed tears was that Grandpa Jean fended off the cold for him by blowing the hot air at the dazhui point. At that moment, Liu Chao felt he had a home in Xi'an, and Jean was his own grandpa! Even now when he remembers that scene, Liu Chao is moved to tears. Hearing that Liu Chao's family had economic difficulties in supporting two college students and one middle school student, Jean bore the expenses for Liu Chao's schooling, so that he could finish his regular college course. When Liu Chao prepared to take the graduate school exam, Jean subsidised him with an extra Rmb800 to cover his living expenses. Liu Chao refused to take it, but Jean insisted. He told Liu Chao: "You need to live." Liu Chao was admitted to be a graduate student of Shaanxi Normal University with the highest mark in 2009. He was wholeheartedly grateful to Grandpa Jean. Without his subsidies and encouragement, he would have hardly finished school, let alone study for a master's degree.

Jean's care for children also extended to their families and friends. In the winter of 2010, Xia Li's father was seriously ill in hospital. At a critical time, when the family was trapped in trouble, Grandpa Jean resolutely gave a helping hand to Xia Li and subsidised Xia Li's father's hospital costs. Afterwards, Grandpa Jean paid the tuition fees for Xia Li for 2011 so that Xia could finish school. Also in 2010, the father of Liu Chao's friend was in hospital and could not afford the medical treatment. Once again, Grandpa Jean offered his help. Grandpa Jean asked these children 'not to publicise' his beneficence, and regarded what he had done as ordinary and not worth mentioning.

Jean offered selfless help to others, but did not pay any attention to the creature comforts. He lived a simple, pure life, based on careful calculation and strict budgeting. For years, he had lived a simple and frugal life and saved the money to help those in need. Jean made a plan for his properties in fine detail, and even specified the use of each Chinese yuan. Apart from buying books, he spent very little on himself but saved most of it to help others. To Jean, it was the most reasonable and most meaningful application of wealth. For years, Jean carefully planned his future life and 'squeezed' out donations. He had no savings, but a bank card from the Bank of China to receive his pension from the French government. The bank card was linked to several charity organisations and part of the money on it would be automatically transferred to all the pre-arranged charities on the day when Jean's pension was received in his account.

Zhang Cheng, who was a companion to Grandpa Jean, till the end of his life said: "His life was quite simple. Apart from books, he had little spending but was generous to others." That was Jean, a man stingy to himself, but generous to others. He was absolutely not mean but selfless. Born to the purple, he never pursued the aristocratic life but cherished benevolent, compassionate feelings of the common people. The character '德' (meaning 'virtue') in the middle of his Chinese name represented the nobility in his blood.

6. Transmitted Great Love in 'Smiles'

In Jean's living room there was an old-fashioned chair, covered in artificial leather, whose surface cracked due to wear. Whenever his friends visited him, Jean would always sit on the chair in the corner of the living room, looked at everyone, smiling, and listened to their free talk. He would carefully and quietly listen to others talk, whether the topic was related to him or not. Jean's smile was full of magic and warmth which bridged spiritual communication. Most of the time, his friends came to visit Jean only to stay longer with him. Without saying a word, Jean's smiles would drive away their difficulties in life. Lu Dong, a friend of Jean for many years, found from the beginning of their acquaintance that Jean would smile to others each time he met them, and then began his work. Initially, Lu Dong did not understand why the foreigner liked smiling so much. Gradually, Lu Dong saw the point. Just as Mother Teresa of Calcutta, Jean's friend and Nobel Peace Prize winner said: "Smiles are the start of love. Once we love each other, we will do something for each other." For decades, Jean's smile vividly and profoundly interpreted Mother Teresa's words. Jean's smile made others feel his kindheartedness and it conveyed his greeting and respect. A smile was his way of making inquiries for life and attracted people to listen to the sound of their life and satisfy their pure demand for life.

One autumn, Michel Grolleaud, a UN agricultural expert, came to Xi'an to visit his old friend Jean. Faded leaves fell on the campus of XISU and the handymen were cleaning the fallen leaves. When Michèle and Jean were about to walk out of the school gate, Jean recognised one of the cleaners and led Michèle towards him. Michèle noticed that the cleaner was tall and wore plain clothes. Concentrating, and due to ill-health and tiredness, he bowed to work. At the sight of Jean and Michèle, the cleaner immediately stood upright. Seeing Jean's tacit smile, his wrinkled face broke into a smile too. When they were about to leave, Jean made eye contact with Michèle and told him that the person they met was a 'kindhearted man' of angelic smiles.

Gifts for Jean from his friends carefully placed on the bookshelf

Jean made true, close friends, in spite of differences in ages, all over the world. His friends were drawn to him not because of his social position but out of their admiration for his personal charisma. Lu Dong and other friends often called Jean and asked whether he needed some daily necessities. Jean always replied, smiling: "I need nothing else apart from you." In the eyes of Jean, nothing was more valuable than friendship in the world, and he made a lifelong pursuit of spiritual wealth and friendship.

Jean calling a friend

Chapter 5
A Passion for China

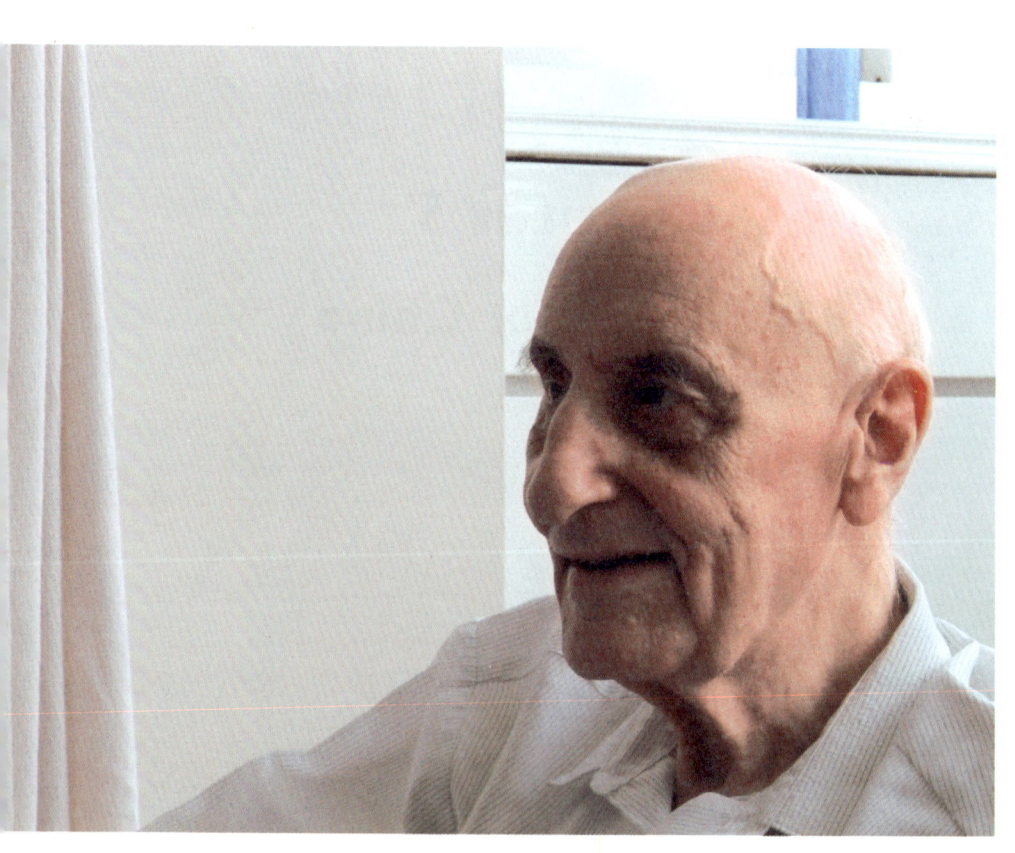

Chapter 5

When he first came to work in the XISU in 1976, Jean lived in the family dormitory building, like other XISU staff. In 1984, when he was about to retire, the university built the foreign faculty residence to improve the accommodation of foreign teachers. For 31 years, Jean lived in Room 401, F2, Unit 1, Foreign Faculty Residence II. Jean was grateful to the Chinese government to grant him the right to permanent residency so that he could settle in China and to XISU for his 'home' there. Whenever his friends came to visit him in his residence, Jean would always say: "Welcome to my home."

Jean spent the latter half of his life in China. For four decades, his love for China, just like wine, did not decrease but grew stronger with the passing days. Jean often enthused to his friends: "I chose China and I made the correct choice. I'm proud to be Chinese!"

1. Service to the Chinese People

In September 1976, Director Wang Kejian of the XISU department of German, French and Spanish, accompanied Jean to visit Yan'an, Shaanxi, shortly after he came to Xi'an. In the old, Communist revolutionary area, Jean knew that Mao Zedong proposed the idea of 'serving the people' in memory of Zhang Side. He sincerely identified with, and liked, that idea, and was determined to practice it with his own actions in order to do something good for ordinary people. It was then that Jean initiated his charity journey in Xi'an and throughout China.

Jean came to Xi'an when he was nearly in his sixties. Still, he often offered his seat to other senior citizens or women on a bus. Once when he was on a bus, a disabled person could not get onto the bus because of the crowd. Jean, being tall, stood at the door and stretched his arms to bar the crowd, shouting loudly: "We should learn from Lei Feng and let him get on the bus first." Jean's action moved those crowding to get on, they stopped and made way for the disabled man to board first.

Before his retirement, Jean often rode his bicycle around the streets, to get familiar with the environment, know the conditions of the people and relieve distress among the poor. He radiated love. Wherever he went, Jean always gave others a sense of warmth. Yao Taer, a teacher at XISU, remembered an incident that happened in 1977. At that time, he and Jean went to attend to some affairs in the city. Jean suddenly got off his bicycle when they came to the south gate. Confused, Yao Taer followed suit and saw that the lid of a sewer was missing and there was a round, black hole, which was deep and frightening. Jean said: "It is too dangerous! We need to make a sign to prevent others from falling into it." After that, Jean placed his bicycle horizontally above the well head of the sewer, found some bricks and built a wall. Seeing that it was safe again, Jean unknitted his brows and smiled.

Jean's good deeds were widely known among the people who regarded him as 'a foreign Lei Feng'. Nevertheless, when a correspondent came to Jean, hoping to interview him, the old man, known for virtue, continuously said no, saying of his acts of kindness: "They were not worth mentioning but what everyone should do!" Jean's close friends knew that Jean disliked others talking about such issues. He never spoke of general principles but took down-to-earth actions. He started with small things, helped others and showed his pursuit for kindness, love and a harmonious society, and his yearning for a beautiful world. He regarded it as his mission and would triumph over anxiety and transmit the positive energy with his strong spirit, even in the face of most serious setbacks. As Xing Zhiqiang said, Jean always empowered others in a subtle, intangible manner and it seemed like warm sunshine or a spring breeze to be in contact with him. Jean's pursuit for a lofty spiritual life aroused people's emotions.

2. Felt the Suffering of the Poor

During his trip to Yan'an, when he initially came to teach at XISU, Jean witnessed the harsh, rural life in China in the later period of the Cultural Revolution. The fact that the farmers toiled hard in the soil deeply touched Jean who actively requested to work with them to experience their painstaking labour. That experience generated the persistent love in Jean for Chinese farmers. To Xia Li, Jean's student, looking after him before his death, Jean found favour with the Chinese people, especially the ordinary Chinese people - the farmers. Jean often said, without the Chinese farmers, there would have been no farming culture, or traditions and culture going back thousands of years.

Jean's care for the Chinese people was also shown in his generosity in the streets of the ancient city of Xi'an. Xi'an Bell Tower, in the centre of Xi'an, and at the crossing of the four streets, leading east, west, south and north within the city walls, was the biggest and best-preserved of the bell towers still left in China. Initially built in the street corner of the present Guangji street in the 17th year of Hongwu Emperor (Taizu) of the Ming dynasty (AD1384), it was erected face to face with the Drum Tower, and relocated to its present site in the 10th year of Wanli Emperor (AD1582). It was a landmark building in Xi'an. Surrounded by prosperous businesses, it was also a gathering place for vagrants and beggars who were the regular recipients of Jean's aid. Even though his friends recognised at a glance that begging was the occupation of some of the beggars, exploiting people's kindness, Jean would persist in helping them financially, regardless of persuasion from his friends. During the decades when he could move about easily, Jean would take with him small change, Rmb5 or Rmb10, and rode his bicycle to the thriving Xiaozhai, or the south gate, where beggars often appeared. He would generously help those in need. Zhang Cheng, who was with Jean in his late years, recalled when Jean and his friends had a meal in Xiaozhai. He did not notice a beggar at the roadside when he helped Jean to go upstairs. After the meal, and arriving home, Jean secretly took a taxi to the overpass in Xiaozhai, gave some money to that beggar and returned home. In winter, Jean would give food and warm clothes to the vagrants hiding in the doorways. When he could not move about easily, due to his age, he asked Zhang Cheng to do this on his behalf. Jean always wore old clothes and would save better clothes for the destitute people he did not know.

One Christmas, it snowed heavily in Xi'an. Jean invited his friends to dine in the Huanghelou (Yellow Crane Tower) Hotel. During the meal, his friends noticed Jean's abnormal demeanour. Jean, usually all smiles, was poker-faced and down-hearted. After returning home, he sat up the whole night on the chair he often sat on in the living room. He began to consider whether he should return to France because, on the way to the hotel, he saw a grey-haired old woman picking up garbage in the snow. Jean felt bitter and was eager to do something for her. Nevertheless, he was also an old man that could not do many things. All of a sudden, he came to awareness that he could no longer do anything for China. He thought overnight and decided to return to France. The next day, his friends, Li Tao and Yang Chenguang, who were worried about Jean, came to see him in his house. After repeated inquiries, Jean spoke of his anguish and discussed with his friends the prospect of returning to France. His friends were stupefied and hated the thought of being parted from Jean. They persuaded and promised him: "We will help you with what you cannot fulfill." Jean smiled and gave up the idea of returning to France, and his bitter facial expressions finally vanished.

3. Heartfelt Help for Chinese Students in the Mountains

Being familiar with Jean, Geng Qiang knew that it was his wish to help the aged and children. He came across the difficulties of education for poverty-stricken children when he worked in Shaanxi province. He had the idea to set up a fund for donations to the schools. It happened that Jean had the same concerns and when Geng Qiang put forward his proposal Jean immediately nodded his support. He promptly decided to donate. Originally, Geng Qiang was unsure about the title of the fund and suddenly thought of '米睿哲', the Chinese name Jean had adopted. He blurted out: "How about 'The Mi Ruizhe Charity Education Foundation'?" Everyone agreed as it reflected Jean's benevolent spirit. They decided to launch the campaign without delay. As well as Geng Qiang, other friends of Jean took part.

Geng Qiang and Liu Chao at Zhongxin primary school, Xihe, Shiquan county, donating student charity grants on behalf of Jean, 8 November 2011

As Jean grew older, he had difficulties in moving around. On 8 November 2011, Geng Qiang, Gong Yongfeng, director general of Xi'an Volunteer Alliance, and Liu Chao, a student of XISU, came to Zhongxin primary school in Xihe, Shiquan county, Ankang city, Shaanxi province, and donated the first student charity grants of Rmb9,840 to 13 students

Chapter 5

and promised to subsidise them so they could finish their education at the primary school, on behalf of Jean.

Jean, in his nineties, thought of these children, and kept a close watch on the studies and lives of the students. On 21 November 2013, Jean entrusted Geng Qiang, Tian Wenke, a volunteer in Xi'an, and his French friends, Pierre Vuong and Annaud, to make the arduous journey to Zhongxin primary school in Xihe, to visit the 13 subsidised students and bring them supplies. They chatted with them, inquired about their studies and lives and encouraged them to study well and be healthy. When his friends brought the children's feedback to Jean, he was extremely happy and wanted to see these children in person, regardless of his age. Before Jean's death, the Mi Ruizhe Charity Education Foundation had donated a total of Rmb20,000 and subsidised the 13 students until their graduation from primary school. Despite having little money, Jean gave all his savings to charity.

Many people saw Jean offer help to others but did not ask why he would help others with such dedication and effort for decades. In addition to his inner quest, was there any external force supporting him to continue? The answer was quite simple. It was friends. As the French saying goes, "You tell me who your friends are, and I know who you are." Jean and his close Chinese friends influenced each other. Jean moved his friends with his

The students of Zhongxin primary school in Xihe, showing their gratitude for Grandpa Jean's help

On 21 November, Pierre Vuong (far right) and Annaud (centre) visiting the students in Zhongxin primary school on behalf of Jean

benevolent actions and influenced everyone around him with his morality and personal charm. Everyone could also experience his kindness and selflessness. Moved and inspired by Jean, his friends, in turn, gave to society with their own actions. Meanwhile, the Chinese people affected Jean with their own actions and felt warmly towards him, so that he gradually took China, his 'second hometown', as his only home. Jean's relatives did not understand his decision to live permanently in China, but when they came to Xi'an and met his Chinese friends, they understood. An elderly man would not normally be surrounded by so many people, but Jean had many friends in Xi'an, who made a large family for him. It was because of them that Jean decided to live in China. Jean lived in Xi'an and Xi'an was his home.

4. The Warmth of the Chinese People

In the second year of teaching at XISU, Jean proposed not to receive a salary from the university, only the subsidies from the French government, because he would "undergo the most difficult period with the Chinese people." After China's economy improved, Jean still refused to be paid by China. He said he would contribute the money to where the money was more badly needed. Jean generously offered financial help using the subsidies granted by the French government to those in need, as well as subsidising Chinese students studying in France, or those near him.

Jean's benevolence influenced many ordinary people, who voluntarily did whatever they could to help this elderly, French man. It was difficult to buy sliced bread, the staple food favoured by Jean, in the 1970s and 1980s. The staffers of the foreign restaurant of XISU bought it especially for Jean in the Xi'an restaurant all the time. Jean stood 1.9m tall, and the quilts sold in the shopping mall did not fit him, failing to cover either his shoulders or his feet. Yang Chenguang's mother sewed an overlong quilt for him by hand, and Jean could finally sleep comfortably at night. Jean's cloth shoes were lovingly sewn by hand by Xia Li's mother and did not wear out for years. Jean appreciated Xing Zhiqiang's exquisite skills and treated him like a son. Xing also revered Jean and regarded him as a father. From 2013, Xing often went to Jean's house to take care of him and to massage him. When Jean needed to take the Chinese medicine for his intestines and stomach, Xing brewed the medicine in his own house every day as Jean did not have an earthenware cooking pot to use. In Jean's last days, Xing was with him. At that time, Jean was rather weak and could not take oral medicine. As a consequence, Xing, who knew a little about TCM through self-study, relieved Jean of pain by applying a plaster onto his navel. Knowing the folklore that washing feet in water with green onion roots could help the free movement of the bowels, Xing used that method to wash Jean's feet. Many friends of Jean had done a lot for him. In addition

Jean in his study at XISU

to looking after him with trivial matters, when Jean needed help for some other issues, due to his age, his friends gave a helping hand, fulfilling his wish, for instance, to continue with Sino-French exchanges, subsidise Chinese students to study in France, give relief to the 'have-nots' and to set up the Mi Ruizhe Charity Education Foundation. It was these Chinese friends that provided for Jean the care of a family. In his essay *'Gratitude of a Westerner'*, he wrote: "My thanks should go to my friends, over 30 years, for their care, help and support. They helped me find out the miracles of China, especially of Xi'an."

Geng Qiang and Yang Chenguang assisting Jean in classifying data

'Everyone has a Confucius in his mind' was the philosophy of Wang Yangming, which formed Jean's understanding of life and stimulated the interaction between Jean and the Chinese people. Jean moved the Chinese people with his benevolence and saw the brilliance of 'essential conscience' in the Chinese, which in turn made him more persistent in his benevolence and to do something in return for the country and its people. Now we can finally understand the source of Jean's admiration of the Chinese culture. Jean held that the brilliance of China lay in the thinkers she had fostered. For instance, Lao Tzu wrote his *Tao Te Ching* on the Louguantai; and doctors, for example Sun Simiao who wrote the enduring *'Formulas Worth a Thousand Gold Pieces'*; artists who created amazing bronzeware terracotta warriors and frescoes. The greatest brilliance, however, was her people, who were filled with incredible wisdom and created countless great wonders. These miracles remain forever in the minds of people around the world.

Chapter 5

5. Admiration for the Self-sacrifice of the Chinese People

Jean cared for and subsidised the ordinary people and praised their spirit of sacrifice. Jean was fond of hearing stories showing the character and good deeds of the Chinese people, narrated by his friends. He repeatedly said he hoped to publish some books about the personalities and deeds of the Chinese and introduce these books abroad. In an essay entitled *The Hidden Chinese Faces*, Jean wrote: "As an 87-year-old living in the 21st century, I find something amazing. Months ago, a 93-year-old Chinese man passed away. He owned a tricycle and lived a simple life. When he was alive, he offered constant financial help to those who could not afford to finish school. What an example of the Chinese people who deserve my admiration and respect!" The senior Chinese man in Jean's essay was Bai Fangli, a Tianjinese who cycled for nearly 60 years to financially support education. He donated Rmb350,000 in total and fulfilled the dreams of 300 poverty-stricken children to finish college study. The elderly man met and saw off passengers at Tianjin railway station every day and focused on those with particular difficulties. On his dilapidated tricycle hung a small red flag with the words 'Half price for families of revolutionary martyrs and servicemen, preferential treatment for the old, weak, sick and disabled and voluntary services for the old and childless' to offer favourable pricing for some passengers. It was just how he did it. He pedalled every day with one foot high and the other low, through wind and rain, from morning till night, and saved each cent made by his toil, and donated all the money to numerous students. During the process of supporting education by pedalling for more than 10 years, Bai Fangli also donated money to China Youth Development Foundation, the 43rd World Table Tennis Championships and the municipal senior people's home. Bai Fangli once told a teacher at Nankai University: "I, old and illiterate, am incapable of making contributions to the country, but the college students I make donations for are quite different. They are educated, they master scientific knowledge, may probably become great talents and contribute more to the country!" and "They should do well in studying, work and conducting themselves and contribute more to the country." That was the simple requirement for the children subsidised by him. His requirement was similar to Jean's for the Chinese overseas students in France he subsidised to 'serve China after graduation'! When he became one of the top 20 candidates for 'The Person of the Year of Touching the Heart of China 2004', selected by China Central Television, Bai Fangli responded: "I've done nothing

Chapter 5

special and do not deserve the attention of the authorities." It reminds us of Jean's usual response: "I've done nothing" and "It's not worth mentioning." The two elderly men, one Chinese and the other French, had not met before but their pursuits accorded with each other simply because they held up high the great love in the world! Bai Fangli did not know that a French man was profoundly touched by him after he passed away, but Jean knew that he should keep up the benevolent dedication of the Chinese man with his own deeds.

In 1998, catastrophic floods burst the Yangtze river, in south China, creating a disastrous situation. Jean kept a close watch on the TV programmes and newspapers every day to keep informed of the latest rescue efforts. At the news that the People's Liberation Army (PLA) fought against floods and saved people, Jean commended the PLA soldiers as saints.

The 12 May 2012 earthquake in Wenchuan, Sichuan province, affected Xi'an to a different extent. Ren Zhanfeng paid a visit to Jean in the foreign faculty residence of XISU on behalf of the university and the department. With his bent back and difficulty in standing up straight, Jean slowly stood up to welcome him. They hadn't met each other for so long. The passing years had seen the stooping of Jean's tall stature, but he still showed his respect for his friend. Jean took out a copy of *Hua Shang Daily*, dated 16 May, and pointed at the report about the Wenchuan earthquake. He wiped tears from his eyes now and then and solemnly said: "Too miserable... too miserable..." After that, he pointed at a photo on the page showing a PLA soldier carrying a child on his back and made a thumbs up sign, commending: "Amazing China! Extraordinary PLA!"

What he experienced, saw, and heard in China over so many years filled Jean with his deep love and high praise for the Chinese. He wrote a poem 'The People of China'[1] in 2013, which was engraved on his tombstone as follows:

> *The closer I approach the Chinese,*
> *The more unsurpassed courage I've found*
> *Through thousands of examples.*
> *The courage comes from the farmers.*

---

[1] **French title:** *Le Peuple de Chine*

> *Despite the scorching heat and the torrential floods,*
> *They toil every day indefatigably with persistence.*
> *The courage comes from the workers,*
> *Who brave all the risks to build the skyscrapers.*
> *The courage is found in the soldiers,*
> *Who sacrificed their lives to save others after the earthquake*
> *Regardless of their personal gains.*

In Jean's view, the farmers labouring all day long, the workers building skyscrapers, and the PLA soldiers saving others at the risk of their own lives, were all among his 'thousands of examples'. The Chinese people around him showed him the country and the people that deserved his deep love. In his poem *'Tribute to the People of China (1969-1999)'*[2], written in 1999, he expressed his ardent love for China, his 'second hometown' in passionate words:

> *30 years of life in the middle of the people of China, 30 years during which it has been given to discover the qualities which have been remarkable from the Chinese.*
>
> *It's the greatest luck for me to see their exquisite hands, their unique ideas and their spiritual treasure.*
>
> *Why don't we exclaim for the exquisite hands of the Chinese?*
>
> *The hands of the TCM doctors can precisely acupuncture some points of the body that are difficult to determine so that the energy or vital essence of life can recirculate and cure the pains of the patients.*
>
> *The hands of the surgeons can deftly connect up the broken wrist or finger and reforge the burnt-out facial features with matchless patience.*
>
> *The hands of the calligraphers and painters can create calligraphic works, portraits and fresco of extraordinary beauty with master hand in a flash.*

---

[2] French title: *Hommage au Peuple de Chine*

Chapter 5

> *The hands of the sculptors can knead the clay and leave such perfect, vivid faces and countenances, as the Qin Shi Huang's Buried Sculpture Legion, for future generations.*
>
> *The hands of the gardeners can meticulously decorate the city's garden and the unit's greenbelt.*
>
> *The hands of the workers and farmers are used to labour in the fields, caves and mines and build high-rise buildings in severely, bitter cold or burning hot weather and with various risks, especially unforgettable in Shanghai.*

Jean said: "I think the Chinese people are exceptionally intelligent, wise and diligent in the world. In particular, that the Chinese people could make gorgeous bronzeware and chinaware very early, astonished me. It thus can be said that it was the exquisite hands, exceptional wisdom and kind hearts of the Chinese people that attracted me to China." The plain sentences of Jean clearly reveal his ardent love for China.

6. Deep Love for China

In the initial stage of the reform and opening up of China, Jean often told his students, colleagues and friends that it would surely succeed, thanks to China's rapid economic growth. At that time, Jean gestured and said in non-standard Mandarin: "China's rocketing economic growth is bound to surpass that of France and other western countries in only a couple of years." Then, his sentences were regarded as ostentatious and just small talk. However, years later, people could finally sense that they were the innermost thoughts and feelings of the aged man. More than 30 years later, China underwent earthshaking, radical changes, just as Jean predicted. People had to admire his sagacity and foresight.

Jean also paid attention to the problems arising due to China's expansion. He still believed in China, and positively and optimistically regarded these problems as inevitable experiences. Once, Jean met with a previous student in France who complained to Jean and criticised China's status quo. Jean did not agree with the student's view and energetically defended China. It seemed to others that the Chinese student was a French man and that Jean was Chinese.

Many of Jean's friends were very impressed by Jean's analogy of a plane taking off to describe China's accelerated development. As Jean said, China was like a plane, taking off at a high speed. It was normal for the passengers to quarrel on the plane, so it was normal and needless to be panicked at any problems encountered amid China's development, and not lose confidence in the country. It was Jean, who gained an insight into the essence of any issue rather than make superficial judgment.

Jean was full of hopes for China at all times because of his deep love for China. He thought: "The Chinese people cherish peace and China has not launched any aggressive wars. Besides, China boasts Lao Tzu and Confucius, reputed for their profound ideology and great wisdom." The oriental country of ancient civilisation was lovely in his heart, but he often criticised the western society into which he was born. Gentility and radicalisation mingled perfectly in Jean. He usually treated others gently and delightfully, but voiced his dissatisfaction with the unreasonable phenomena in western countries, especially some inappropriate behaviours advocated by governments, such as materialism.

He spoke highly of China's reform and opening up policy but often criticised the French government. He was indignant in particular about the improper actions of the French government in handling the key problems during Sino-French exchanges. After French President Nicolas Sarkozy met the Dalai Lama, Jean immediately wrote an email criticising President Sarkozy and mobilised his friends in France to launch a 'signature campaign' to oppose the President. The action of President Sarkozy and the French government was a monstrous diplomatic error, and he criticised the French government for being "extremely stupid" and said it should "get a spanking".

When the Olympic torch relay in Paris, in 2008 was thwarted by some Tibetan independence supporters, this gave rise to discussion of the French people. In Jean's view, the one-sided publicity of the French news outlets hid the truth concerning the China issue to the French public. In his words, they "had no idea of the truth". That issue worried Jean. Zhu Weimin, an orthopedist who had studied in France with a grant from Jean, worked in a hospital in France. He hurriedly called Jean to tell him how he explained to the French people around and helped them to know the truth in France. Jean praised Zhu Weimin

Chapter 5

for that and said: "France needs a myriad of doctors like you." Zhu understood what Jean meant, that is to say, the French people badly needed that help.

Years before, Jean hoped that Zhu Weimin could return to China and serve the Chinese people as he stipulated to Chinese students studying in France with his subsidy. Zhu Weimin, however, lived in France for some special reasons. Jean did not impose his will on Zhu and only said: "It's up to you!" Zhu Weimin understood that Jean was judging him, but Jean found from that incident that students in France could do something for China, and France also needed some Chinese people, as the envoys of Sino-French exchanges and as the bridge of friendship between the two peoples. He felt relieved at last. Jean loved China so much that he thought China's fate was closely bound up with his and he thought of China wholeheartedly!

Jean was a professional teacher who detested arbitrary educational charges and would lament this to his former colleagues and leaders of XISU almost every time he met them. He often showed sympathy to the poor students in the rural areas, and insisted that they should not be charged for education lest their talents should be stifled. Jean felt happy knowing that the school children in the poorest areas were benefiting from the 'free lunch' campaign, with the advocacy and help of some charities. The campaign was a non-governmental, public-benefit programme, jointly initiated by more than 500 correspondents, including Deng Fei, domestic media and the China Social Welfare Foundation (CSWF), through which Jean sensed the kindness and solidarity of the Chinese people. Additionally, he was averse to corruption he saw or heard from the news media, and was too worried about the coal miners dying in mining disasters to have a meal. He often asked his friends about living conditions, wages and job security of the migrant workers, and paid close attention to their demands for payments and safeguards for their legal rights. He nodded with understanding and satisfaction after learning that the government was settling, and protecting, the legal rights and interests of the migrant workers.

Jean had the heartfelt and genuine friendship of the Chinese people, so Jean remembered and appreciated the good deeds of many leaders of China because "they love the people and the people love them. They laugh when the people laugh and cry when the people cry. They are all very great national leaders, especially Zhou Enlai whose thoughts and actions exemplified the principles of the present harmonious society..." To Jean, it was 'amazing progress' for China to offer universal medical insurance, solve the difficulties of getting medical service, and introduce exemption from agricultural taxation. He said: "I've noticed China's development during so many years. China is the hope of the world."

At one time, Jean was worried about some of China's changes, for instance, the high-rise buildings and the money-based changes, and feared that China should lose its correct direction of advancement. In 1994, Michel Grolleaud, Jean's friend and UN agricultural specialist, paid a visit to China and came to Xi'an to see Jean. Jean took him to the terracotta warriors, for the second time. Unlike their first visit in 1987, they were badgered with groups of young people touting souvenirs for tourists. Jean refused, smilingly at first, but became impatient and vexed later by their repeated, forceful selling, and finally 'burst out'. He shouted loudly in Chinese: "I've had it!" and then told Michèle: "Let's go into the exhibition hall." Evidently, the commercialisation caused Jean's aversion, because he predicted the change in the development of mass tourism. In his view, the changes sharply went against the purity and nobility of China's recovered national dignity. He told Michèle: "If things go on like that, China will soon lose its soul." Jean's anxieties hit the mark of China's numerous

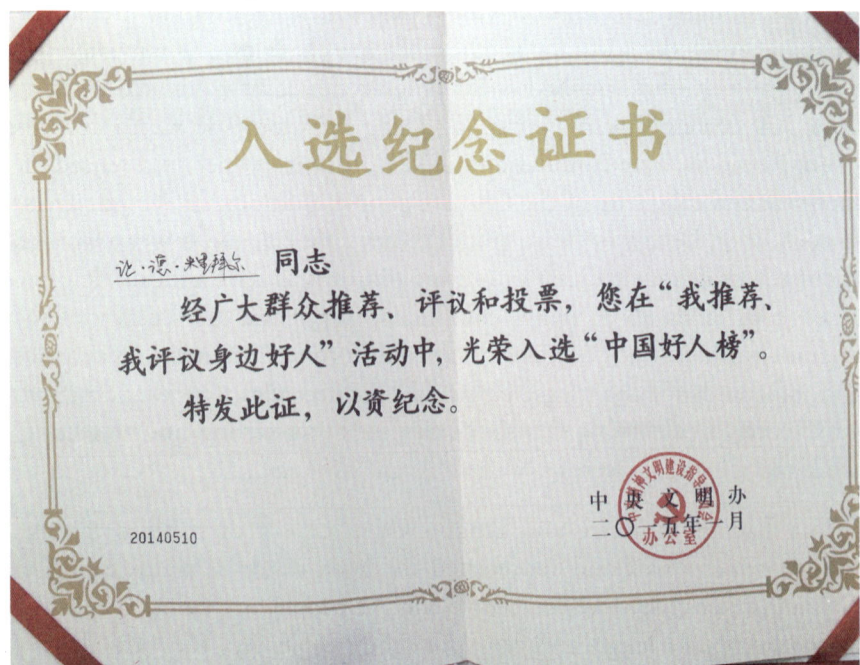

Jean's 'A Person Who has Performed Good Deeds for China' certificate

Chapter 5

problems amid its present social growth. He earnestly hoped the country he loved so much could grow in a sound way. When a significant majority of people only cared for, and focused on, their personal gains and losses, he, as always, zeroed in on how to bring more beauty to the world.

Jean was philanthropic. As a French man, he had the heart of someone from China! On 5 August 2014, the list of the 'My Recommendation and Review of People Who Have Done Good Deeds for China' campaign, sponsored by the Central Civilisation Office and organised by www.wenming.cn, was announced. Jean was among the candidates, following the recommendation of Shaanxi province, and was granted the title of 'Person Who Has Performed Good Deeds for China'. It was his 95th birthday.

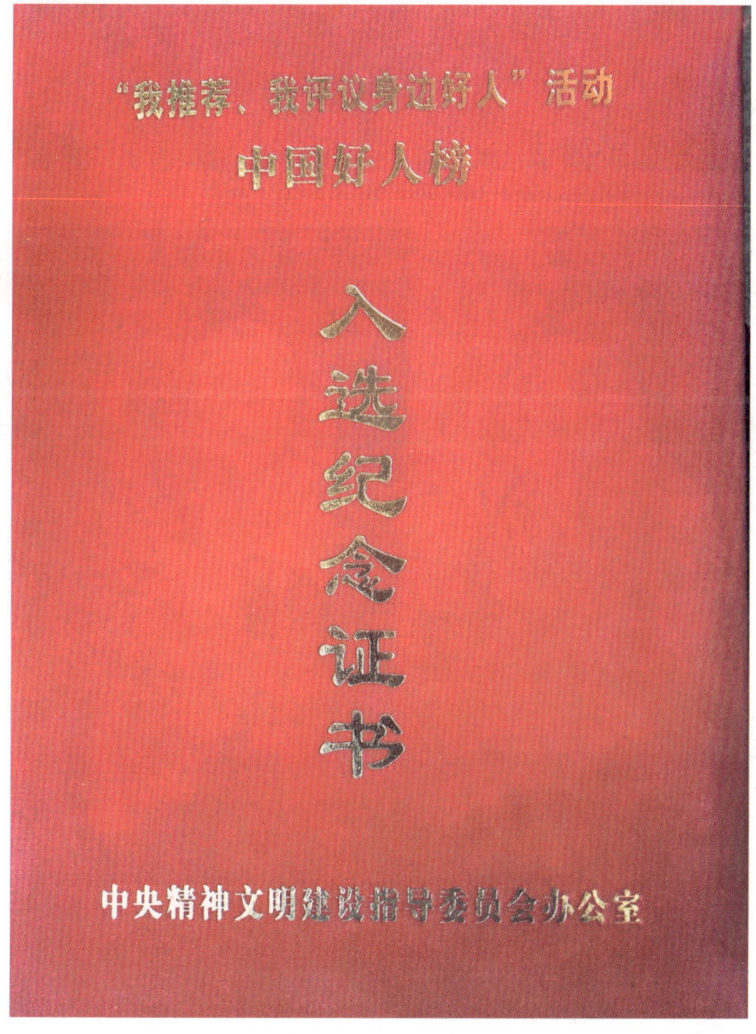

Jean's friends celebrating his 90th birthday on 5 August 2008

Sun Tianyi, former president of XISU, coming to celebrate Jean's 90th birthday in August 2008

Chapter 5

Jean's family and XISU leaders in Xi'an in October 1980

Lu Dong (third from right) and Li Gang (third from left) accompanying Jean and his family along the Yellow River

Jean, his sister and Ma Xi in Xi'an

Jean's nephew in Xi'an

Jean and Cui Shengrui, a cook at XISU

Jean and his friends at Wolong temple in Xi'an

Chapter 5

Jean giving a book to Dr. Yang Chenguang

Jean and Dr. Wang Liqun

Chapter 6

Resting in Peace in His Second Home, China

Jean had to admit he facing the unmerciful time and tide, and advancing in age. "Sorry, I'm getting on in years" was his pet phrase in his later years. However, he struggled on, persistently.

1. His Twilight Years

Each winter morning, Xing Zhiqiang was accustomed to taking morning exercise. He jogged on the playground and always saw a window in the foreign faculty residence where warm light shone like a lonely beacon amid the surrounding pitch-dark, bleak windows. Under the light, sat Jean in front of his computer with reading glasses on, browsing the news and trends, getting information on the major or minor events of China or the world and sending emails to communicate and exchange views on the current political situation with his friends outside China. It was the first thing Jean did in his declining years after he got up at 5:00 each morning, in both winter and summer, year after year. His notebook computer was a gift from 40 French friends and relatives who jointly raised money to buy it to celebrate his 80th birthday. Jean said it was the best birthday gift he'd ever received because it served as the channel for a senior Jean, having difficulties in getting about to communicate with the outside world. From then on, reading internet news and sending emails to his friends became the most important thing for him to do.

Although Jean's inability to walk confined him to the small house, his soul and mind were not restrained. With the help of the internet, Jean maintained close contact with the outside world. Jean was nothing like a man of 70 years old. Diligent and agile in his thinking, and logical, Jean still had his unique, sagacious insight into many issues. Yang Chenguang once asked Jean why he did not get old as quickly and obviously as some senior Chinese men. Jean responded: "Because a man should have objectives to live on." The precious Taoist spirit of continuous reproduction and endless succession could be manifestly seen in Jean.

Jean in his eighties was often seen to stoop over the rough writing desk to arrange the overseas study of Chinese students and apply for scholarships for them, constantly complaining of the small proportion of scholarships granted by the French government to Chinese overseas students. By then, Jean, who had shouted loudly, 'fighting' all his life, sensed his

Chapter 6

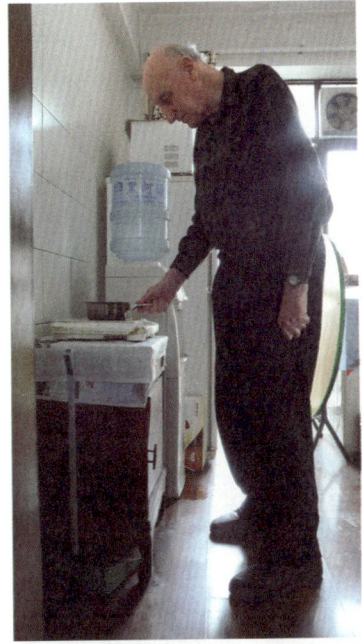

Jean, boiling black tea in the kitchen, pictured right, for his friends

Jean's tableware, neatly placed in his kitchen

A scene from Jean's balcony

powerlessness. He said he was getting on in years and unfamiliar with the latest information and the personages concerned in France, including those of the French embassy in China and he could not do much to help young Chinese to go abroad for further education. His sentences implied his sincere helplessness and unease and he could not rest assured for the world, and for those who he loved most. In his nineties, usually the years when others have one foot in the grave, Jean took his last painstaking efforts to write manuscripts for the study of Liu Chao and Xia Li who were taking care of Jean. He treated them like his own children, teaching them French. Jean also mobilised his friends, including the famous French translator Guo Taichu, and French teachers, Yang Song, Jia Baojun and Hou Xuemei, to encourage and help Liu Chao and Xia Li with their studies. Liu Chao and Xia Li majored in English, but Jean thought that "mastering two languages must fuel a future career to take off!"

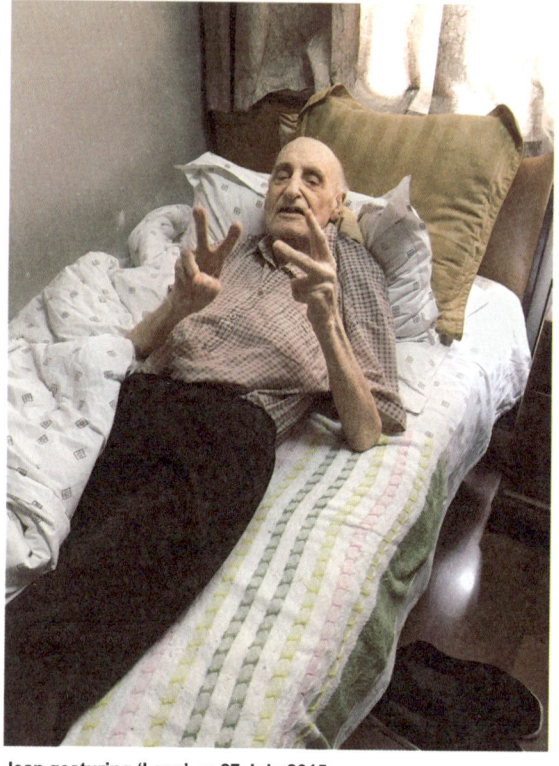

Jean gesturing 'I can' on 27 July 2015

Jean had persistently kept an independent lifestyle for years and, before being bed-bound, did his washing and cooking rather than troubling others. Although the XISU students and friends were worried that something might happen and Jean would be unable to get about at night, and they wanted to stay around him and take care of him around the clock, Jean declined their goodwill. In the winter of 2013, illness seized Jean who refused to be admitted to hospital but took to his bed for rehabilitation at home with students and friends looking after him by turns. Jean felt grateful and sorry for them. Only two weeks later, Jean's condition had improved and he asked them to return home and he continued to take care of himself.

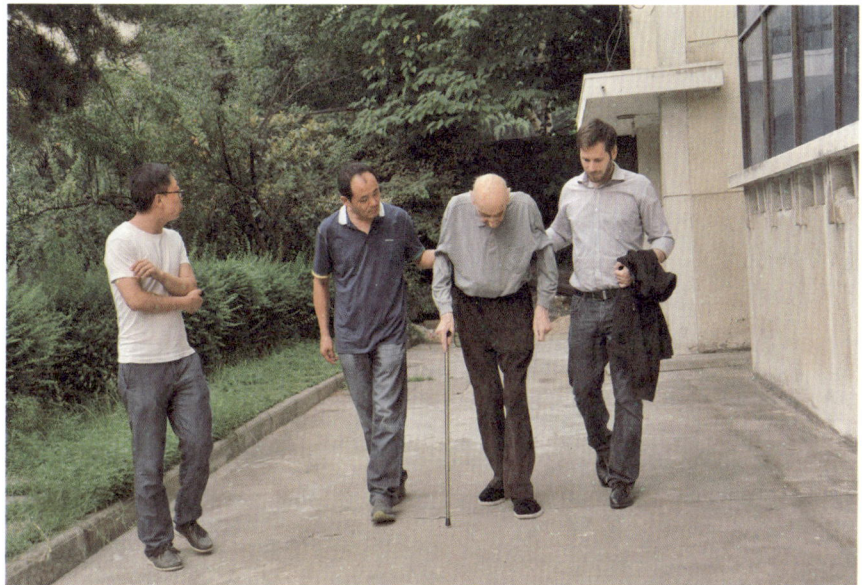

Jean attending the birthday celebration held for him by his friends, 8 August 2015

Jean's friends arriving to celebrate his birthday on 8 August 2015

Everyone had no other alternative but to follow the will of the 'stubborn elderly man'. Nevertheless, they could not rest assured. So they gave him an emergency mobile phone, put it in a small cloth bag and hung it around Jean's neck. The mobile phone had several shortcut keys corresponding to the numbers of his close friends.

A group photo of Jean and his friends at his birthday party on 8 August 2015

On 8 August 2015, Jean telling former Deputy President Liu Yuelian (first from left) of XISU: "I follow the arrangement of God."

They kept their mobile phone power on for 24 hours a day so that they could come to see Jean any time. Jean still wore it around his neck until he passed away. The leaders of XISU also cared for Jean and had several emergency buttons installed at the bedside table, desk, bathroom and kitchen in his house. Once, Wang Bin and Pan Meimei accidentally touched an emergency button when they cleaned Jean's house. Two waitresses from the foreign affairs centre rushed there, thinking something had happened to Jean. However, Jean seldom called his friends at dead of night and almost never used those emergency buttons because he did not want to bother or trouble others.

Jean's bedroom

Jean's clothes were simple and old, but always clean and decent. When his friends, especially female friends, came to see him in his house, he would be dressed neatly to meet his friends. Even though he was ill in bed, he would ask his friends to wait a minute at the door until he put on his suitably decent clothes. Jean's nobility was not shown in his food and clothes but in his words and actions. The chopping board Jean used for more than 30 years was old and shabby but the forks and spoons were always neatly placed on it with care. This showed his cultivation and self-restraint.

2. His Last Days

Haematuria struck Jean in June 2015. At the news, his friends hurried to look after him. Jean had told his friends years before that he would not be admitted to hospital because he would not waste money for one thing, and did not want to stand the torture of mechanical therapy for another. Jean's illness however was very serious and he had to be sent to the hospital for treatment. At this, gentle Jean argued with his friends and said: "I'm getting on in years, but I am not a patient!"

Geng Yiwen and Grandpa Jean in December 2014

Yang Xingjian (left), son of Yang Chenguang, drawing a portrait of Grandpa Jean, 8 August 2010

Chapter 6

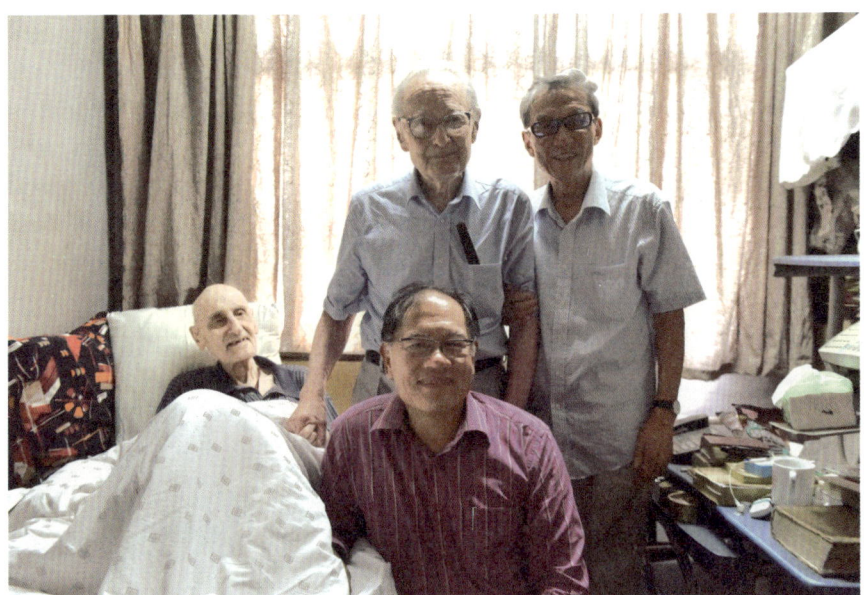

Professor Léon Vandermeersch on a special trip to China from France to see Jean, 1 September 2015

Just like a candle in the wind, Jean's health could not be cured without leaving some effects. After his health improved, he persisted in staying at home. Jean, at that time, was completely bedridden and depended on his friends to help him with many things, which was the last thing he wanted. When his friends proposed to attend to him around the clock, Jean refused as always, saying: "You have your own family to take care of and I can take care of myself. You don't need to be there with me." But this time his friends did not give in, but told him: "You are also my family member" and persisted in waiting on him. To take better care of Jean, his friends hired two professional nursing assistants.

The students originally looking after Jean gave their task top priority. Zhang Cheng took the greatest pains to attend to Jean. He had graduated 10 years before, but purposefully rented a house on the campus of XISU to take care of Jean more conveniently. In the last six months of Jean's life, Zhang Cheng was 'on duty' beside Jean almost every evening. Bedridden for a long time and accustomed to sleeping on his back, Jean developed bedsores. Dr. Yang Chenguang often rushed to Jean's house after work and treated him with moxibustion. Liu Chunhui went out of his way to prepare an air bed for Jean. Zhang Xiaohui and his wife often cooked and sent Jean's favourite soup to him. Jia Zhenfan went to Jean's house to see him first thing every morning. Xing Zhiqiang came to massage and wash his feet and externally apply TCM and relieve Jean of pain. Geng Qiang trimmed Jean's nails and shaved his beard, as if he were serving his own grandfather. The friends prepared a small notebook and everyone on duty was responsible for recording all the details of Jean's life, covering meal times, charting drinking and medicine taking and noting blood pressure measurements. They all attended to Jean patiently and meticulously. On Jean's bedside wall were thickly dotted hand prints of different sizes, left because Jean's pillow was higher and the carers had to support his head with their hands, or help him turn over.

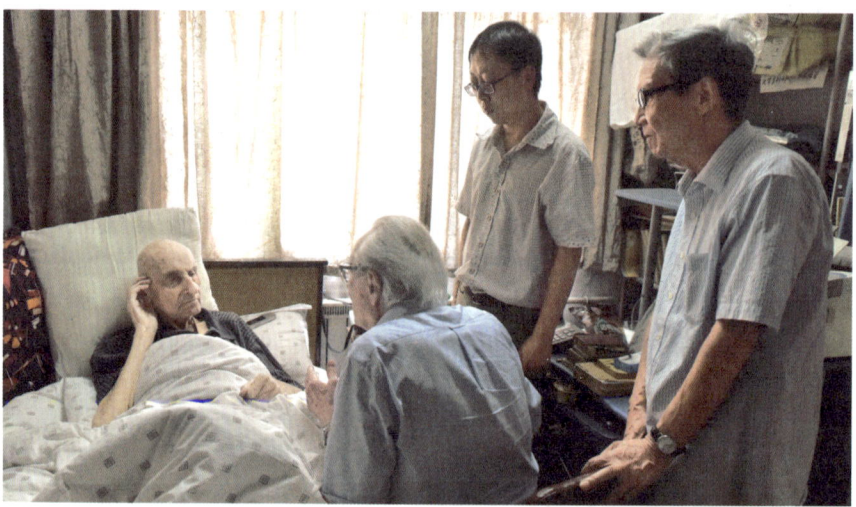

Lu Dong (first from right) and Jia Baojun (second from right), accompanying famous Sinologist Léon Vandermeersch, on a visit to see Jean on 1 September 2015

Watching these 'dutiful children' on the go around his sickbed, Jean often said with regret: "My dear, you are fostering my sloth." Considering these friends could not stay with their families because of him, Jean felt guilty and said: "You should send my sincere thanks to your wife, children and other family members for allowing you to look after me." In his last six months, Jean often asked for his most trusted and most intimate friends, and said to them: "I'm getting on in years. I'm now your burden. I want to leave the world and arrange for my future." The 'future' Jean referred to was after his life, but his friends persuaded him not to indulge in flights of conjecture, and told him: "We are so happy with you there. You're not our burden and we need you so much."

His friends hung a small bedside bell for Jean which would make a loud sound when it rang, so that Jean could wake up the watcher 'on night duty'

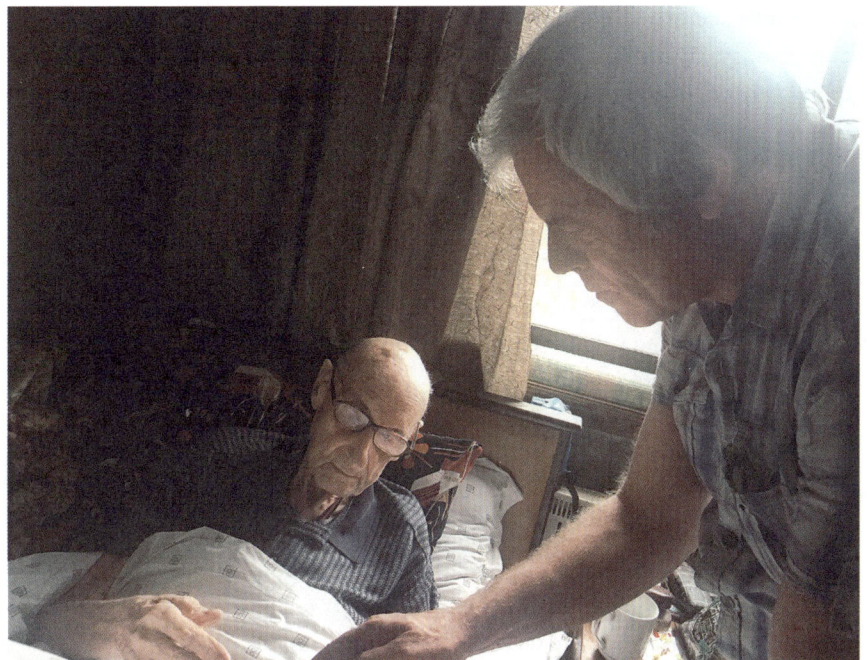

Jean's French friend, Alixan, visiting him on 9 September 2015

in the living room when needed. Jean seldom used it, however, because he did not want to disturb the sleep of friends. He knew that they worked hard in the daytime and hoped that they could have a good rest at night. Once, Geng Qiang was roused from sleep and found that Jean had fallen on the floor of the bathroom; another time, Geng Qiang heard a mild sound in the kitchen. Opening his eyes, he saw that Jean had groped his way to the kitchen, boiled black tea at 5:00 in the morning and prepared breakfast for them. When he could act on his own, he did not let his friends do what he could manage to do, but struggled to his best to take care of himself, and even others.

Jean often had a late night. When he enjoyed good health, he spent time in the quiet nights reading, learning, thinking, researching and writing. The image of Jean wearing his glasses reading and writing under the old lamp with a green lampshade in those days lingered permanently in the memory of Hu Sishe. In the mind of Hu Sishe, former president and student of XISU, Jean was a night watcher and guardian angel of XISU. After he was confined to bed due to serious illness, Jean asked his friends not to turn off the light when he slept at night. In order to let his friends who were looking after him rest, Jean would ostensibly say he was to sleep and ask his friends to keep the door of the bedroom unlatched. When his friends went to see him secretly, he would be staring at the ceiling and lost in thought. Even though in the last stage of his life, his eyes were clear and he still kept an alert mind. He kept on studying and thinking without any let up.

Jean's family members, friends and XISU's representatives discussing Jean's health in his house on 11 September 2015

Jean signing the document for body donation on 20 August 2013

Although he could not sit at his desk to find out about the outside world through his computer and the internet each morning like before, Jean still managed to sit on the bed reading newspapers, or he asked Zhang Cheng or his other friends to read newspapers for him in a bid to be well informed. Being advised to have a rest, he would say: "My dear, you're fostering my sloth" in a tone that said he would not like his friends to spend too much time and energy attending to him. September 2015 was the last month Jean stayed on earth. One day in a newspaper, he saw a photo of a three-year-old Syrian boy, named Aylan, dead on a beach. He felt so pained that he shed tears and immediately asked his close friends to take anything of his that could be donated, including his food and clothes, to the streets to help those in need. As for himself, he refused to use disposable nursing mats to save money, nor did he want to bother his friends to do cleaning for him, so he managed to hold back the desire to defecate. After that, Jean's illness worsened.

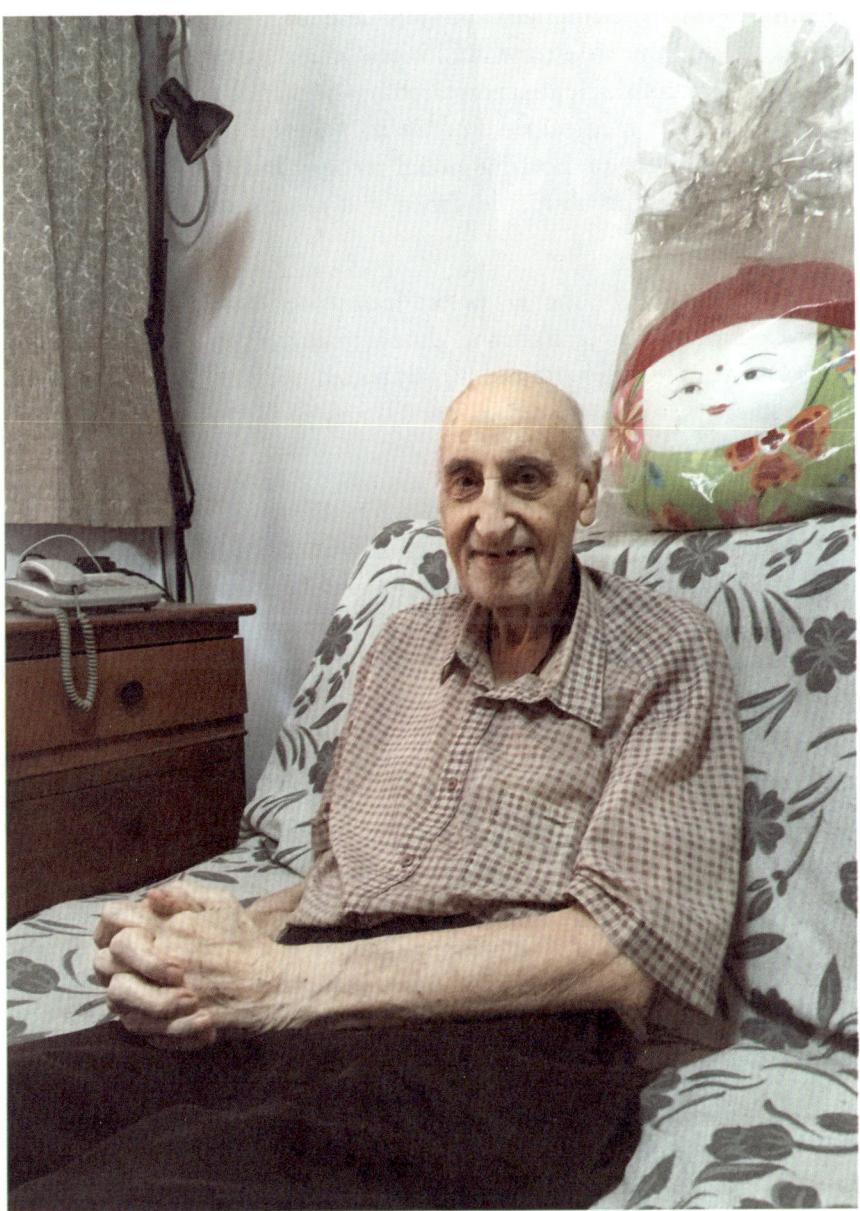

Jean at home, 26 July 2015

On 5 October 2015, Karolinska Institutet of Sweden announced in Stockholm that Tu Youyou, a female Chinese pharmacist and the principal researcher of the Institute of Chinese Materia Medica China Academy of Chinese Medical Sciences, who discovered artemisinin could effectively lower the death rate of malaria patients, received the Nobel Prize in Physiology or Medicine 2015 together with Irish scientist William Campbell and Japanese organic chemist Satoshi Omura. It was the first time a Chinese scientist had won the Nobel Prize in Sciences for scientific research in China itself. It was by far the top award for the medical field of China. It was a pity that Jean, who had been positively supporting global recognition of TCM to benefit the world, had to lie on his deathbed and not share the exciting and joyful news.

On 9 October 2015, the day before Jean passed away, Geng Qiang, as usual, carefully shaved Jean's beard. Unable to utter a syllable, Jean watched Geng Qiang, raised his hand and slightly patted him on the shoulder. Geng Qiang knew that Jean wanted to say: "Thank you! You're so kind to me. Thanks a lot!" just like before.

At about 14:00 on 10 October 2015, the French man closed his eyes and serenely died in his home, a small apartment in the foreign faculty residence of XISU, where he'd lived for 31 years. With his lips closed tight, he looked like a baby sound asleep. Xing Zhiqiang, who stayed with Jean at that time, said Jean's body was warm and soft until the end of his life. At the news that Jean passed away, his friends paused their work and, without delay, rushed from their homes, offices, and even meetings to accompany their dearest Jean for the last moment.

Apart from six months, Jean would live and work in China for a total of 40 years. Unmarried and childless, Jean lived alone but was not lonely. He was never lonely in China and his friends, ranging from more than 90 years old to teenagers, had formed a large family of five generations during those 40 years. His Chinese friends were his family members who always looked after him, comforted him and accompanied him till the last minute of his life.

His friends were silent in his home. The panoramic serenity seemed to have halted time. In a trance, they felt Jean did not lie on the bed but sat on the chair covered by artificial leather in the living room as usual watching all of them with his unforgettable smile…

Chapter 6

Jean, his family and friends in Tongyuan town, Gaoling county, Xi'an, November 2011

3. Fostering Later Generations

Before his birthday in 2013, Jean declared his astonishing decision to donate his body to a Chinese medical institution. It was his choice after thorough consideration. Although they felt shocked, Jean's friends knew that it was quite normal for Jean. "Love, until the last minute" depicted his benevolent disposition. Hearing this, they all shed silent tears and were shocked and moved by Jean's great and holy soul!

In filling out the body donation application form, Jean asked Dr. Yang Chenguang how to write the aspiration of the body donor. Yang told him, "I'm willing to donate my body to China's medical undertaking." After pausing for thought, Jean shook his head and refused. He wanted to write "I hope my body will do a little to help the Chinese doctors". When Jean lowered his head and wrote it carefully, Yang Chenguang immediately shot the scene and has it on his mobile phone, even now.

Through prudent recollection and consideration, Jean detailed his will and made repeated changes to dispose of his belongings. He entrusted his friends, including Wang Bin, Ma Xi, Guo Taichu, Duan Xianglong, Yang Chenguang and Yin Baoku with his cash, savings and negotiable securities, to help orphans and widows and patients who could not afford medical expenses in China.

Jean's body donation application form

Chapter 6

Jean's body donation certificate

Jean's belongings included all the books on the bookshelves, all the things in the bottom drawer of the bedside table, an air-conditioner, a washing machine, a telephone, a microwave, an induction cooker, a tape recorder, a humidifier, a heater, a notebook computer and matching printer and scanner, a loudspeaker box, a desktop computer, a medical kit, two wardrobes, a square table, a wooden coffee table, clothes, shoes and hats in wardrobes, kitchenware and gifts from his friends. Most of these articles were pasted with paper slips reading 'to ...'. Jean had begun doing this years before. Jean started to write his will when he was about 80 years old, and made modifications every one or two years, according to the changed conditions. It was Jean's attitude towards life and also his mental state.

Most of his possessions were books. He hoped: "My dearest friends can choose the books they need". On the gift shelf, the gifts treasured by Jean should "be taken away by the friends who like them". The articles of daily use originally given by his friends, such as the TV, wooden coffee table and humidifier, should be taken away by the givers. Jean also arranged in detail for the recipients of his other articles to express his thanks for their long-term care. He entrusted Doctors Yang Chenguang and Yin Baoku to donate his clothes, shoes and hats in the wardrobes on his behalf. He left all his belongings to the people who he always loved and cared for. We receive profound meaning from his short will: benevolent Jean still cared for those in need even at the end of his life; grateful Jean did not forget others' care for him till his last breath, even though their care could not be compared with what he gave to others; Jean lived an utterly destitute life in terms of material things; he also lived a rich life in terms of spirit. His research on various topics, and his books on the shelves in front of the walls, were all his priceless treasures and spiritual wealth. He lived 'a spiritually rich life of an intellectual'; Jean was detached because he well knew everything was nothing but the vanity of life, and there would then be nothing to care for or worry about…

Jean's family members arriving from France on 12 October 2015

Jean's family members attending the memorial service for Jean and the body donation ceremony on 14 October 2015

Representatives of Jean's family and XISU signing the certificate of authorisation for body donation in March 2016

The teachers and students of XISU holding memorial services before the monument to Jean on Tomb Sweeping Day 2016

Jean always said: "Don't waste anything." In handling his possessions, his friends found many articles they had sent him, including some clothes and food which were brand new and unopened, yet, the checked shirts and shoes Jean often wore had long been worn out and his leather shoes had been beyond repair. In the depth of his wardrobe, his friends found a pair of new cloth shoes made long before by Xia Li's mother. Jean was too fond of them to wear them. After he passed away, his friends could finally put on the cloth shoes for him. In the memory of Li Tao, Jean had a photo which impressed him significantly. It showed Jean from behind, slowly moving ahead with the support of two friends. Li Tao said it was his impression of Jean, "just advance in the way of life." Therefore, although we shed tears for his death, we could do nothing else but to watch his shadow and wished him a smooth journey to the unknown world.

The memorial service for Jean and the body donation ceremony held in Xi'an Jiaotong University Health Science Centre on 14 October 2015

According to Jean's will, his body was donated to Xi'an Jiaotong University Health Science Centre on 14 October 2015. Jean with this practical action carried out his promise to devote the rest of his life to China; a lifelong love without any reservation. A paragraph in *The People of China* written by Jean, ended with a sentence in the *Tao Te Ching*: "The alive not losing their spirit can live longer and the dead not losing their spirit can enjoy longevity." Jean made it. Although his human body vanished, his spirit lived forever in the world! Influenced by Jean, Lu Dong and his wife Cheng Tianzhang, who long admired Jean, decided to donate their bodies after their deaths. Lu Dong said: "We'd like to turn into a handful of clay and stay in the advancing footprints of Jean forever." Xing Zhiqiang wrote an elegiac couplet for Jean: "Leaving his strength of character to inspire the cultural successors, and donating his body out of saintlike kindness". Ingenious Xing made a chrysanthemum with ring-pull cans and polymethyl methacrylate by hand. He said, flowers generally withered, except this one which resembled Jean's spirit. Feder, vice consul of the French embassy in Beijing, commented on Jean:

"Jean was a man of belief. He took roots in Xi'an, not only donating his body to China but also leaving his spirit to China and dedicating all his life to China."

On 22 October 2015, the 12th day after Jean passed away, Geng Qiang et al, as entrusted by Jean, returned to Zhongxin primary school in Xihe town, Shiquan county, and added 10 children from destitute families as recipients for the Mi Ruizhe Charity Education Foundation in China, and granted each of them Rmb1,200 as charity student subsidies. The donation of Rmb12,000 was left by Jean for these children who did not know that the Grandpa Jean they had never met before still cared for them and wanted to see them in person, even before his death. Although he has passed away, his friends will carry on his wishes and go on supporting the Mi Ruizhe Charity Education Foundation in China and even form the 'one-to-one' aid model to help more children finish their studies.

The benevolent sage, envoy and traveller was held in the utmost awe and respect by his admirers. His name, Jean de Miribel (Mi Ruizhe) will be engraved in the mind of the Chinese people.

Jean's death captured much attention in the domestic and overseas media, such as *Nouvelles d'Europe*, China Central Television, *People's Daily*,

The monument to Jean on the Yanta campus of XISU

Chapter 6

the Shaanxi television station, *Shaanxi Daily* and *Xi'an Daily*. The CCTV-10 Science and Education Channel dispatched reporters to Xi'an to find stories about Jean. It made a 40-minute feature programme six months after he passed away to narrate the stories of Jean de Miribel, a 'person who has performed good deed for China' which caused a stir.

People mourned his death. After news of his death spread to France, his former residence in the 13th arrondissement in Paris, saw Chinese people in an endless stream bow and sob with deep emotion. They were the Chinese students, in their fifties or sixties, who had gone to study in France with subsidies from Jean. Despite the passing of time, they would not forget the kindness of Jean.

On 13 October 2015, the evening before the memorial service for Jean, his close Chinese friends and Pierre Vuong, who hurried from France to bid farewell to Jean, gathered in Jean's house. Pierre Vuong delivered a funeral oration at the memorial the next day. Just like the major occasions when Jean delivered speeches, Pierre Vuong made careful preparation: he marked each Chinese character in the oration script with the tones of Chinese pinyin and read aloud while repeatedly choking with sobs before Jean's friends. During Pierre Vuong's oration, past events with Jean brought tears to the eyes of Jean's friends...

Vice Consul Feder of the French embassy in Beijing, attending the memorial service for Jean and the body donation ceremony on 14 October 2015

Jean's family giving an interview on 14 October 2015

Jean's friends going through his possessions, 16 October 2015

Chapter 6

Jean's family members sifting through Jean's books and other belongings which were donated to XISU

Epilogue
Jean's Influence Continues Today

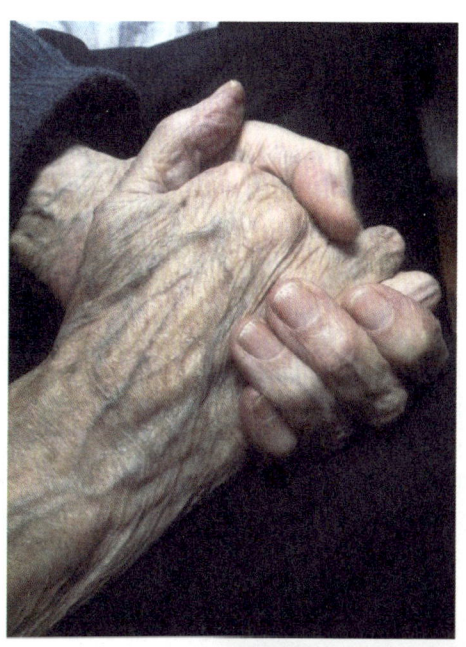

At 10 o'clock on 14 October 2015, the memorial service and the body donation ceremony for Jean de Miribel, a world-noted scholar, lifelong honourary professor of XISU, recipient of the Legion d'Honneur and recognised as 'A Person Who Has Performed Good Deeds for China', was held in the body donation hall of Xi'an Jiaotong University Health Science Centre. Accompanied by sombre funeral music, many people, Jean's family members, friends and colleagues and those who Jean had helped during his lifetime, bade him farewell. They expressed their grief too at the loss of a noble character and respectable spirit, with flowers and tears. Watching the scene, people could not help wondering why did a French man leave his homeland, come to a faraway, oriental, ancient country and dedicate the latter half of his life, about 40 years, to China? Why did a well-travelled, world-famous scholar, who had been to tens of countries and territories, finally choose Xi'an, China and spread his wisdom and care there? Why did a French man of blue blood live a rigourously simple life but donate all his money and belongings to the poor people around him? These questions constantly stirred up our souls and we could not help respecting the man.

Jean often said: "It was the exquisite hands, unexceptional wisdom and kind heart that attracted me to China." He also said: "The Chinese people cherish peace and China has not launched any aggressive wars. I'm proud that I'm a Chinese!" He once cheered in spite of himself: "Long live the heroic, wise and sagacious China!" He took a fancy to China, regarded China as his second hometown and held deep love for the Chinese people. Now let's appreciate the poem neatly written by the senior French man in Chinese characters:

Original Chinese version:

走近中国人

就是追溯

人类

最古老的根源

也是探寻数千年历史

……

走近中国人

就是探索上天赋予这个民族惊人的智慧

其卓越的思想早已让历史流芳

……

Epilogue

Translation:

To get close to the Chinese
Is to retrieve
The oldest origin
Of mankind
And to quest the history of thousands of years
....
To get close to the Chinese
Is to explore the amazing wisdom endowed by God of the nation
Whose excellent thinking has left a good fame in history
....

The simple verses precisely reveal why the senior French man loved China so much. With deeper attachment to China, he loved, understood and extolled China as great, even more than some Chinese. It was the China heart of an elderly French man. From September 1976 to October 2015, he wrote a benevolent, dedicated song to compliment the land of China, in the latter half of his life. Jean's stories were the most touching ones of China. The senior French man, having been through the vicissitudes of life, told the common people with his life what life was and how to spend a life.

A general survey of Jean's life shows that he integrated the noble temperament of the French with the Confucianism and Taoism of China and developed his unique charm. In Jean's world, life was dedication, care and compassion; in the view of others, he was a person transcending the national boundary and nationalities and a kind, noble and pure man. With lofty moral sentiments, rigourous scholarship, a spirit of utter devotion and broad and profound internationalism, Jean integrated the essence of the traditional Chinese culture of "kindheartedness, justice, loyalty, remission, neighbourliness, self-restraint and inner concentration" into the depth of his soul. His stories in China were significantly moving and his noble quality deserves immense admiration. Just as Lu Dong, Jean's good friend during his lifetime, said, "He changed his life into the torch held up high by Prometheus that lit up the road for people's lives, pointed out the right path and functioned as the coordinate of life ahead."

The French man has left us, but his stories in China have not ended.

Just as Lu Dong said: "Jean's good deeds exemplified the process in which the human culture changed human beings. The life of Jean changed many people, especially the Chinese people. Just like the tip of an iceberg, his stories have just begun.

We believe that the undertaking of French education in XISU, established with the help of Jean, with his wisdom and knowledge will embrace constant development and cultivate more French talents; the Chinese culture worshiped by Jean must be carried forward; the Sino-French friendship fostered by Jean for decades must flourish continuously for latter generations, with his influence. Especially, Jean influenced countless people around him with his noble personality and benevolence for decades, and his spirit and personality have deeply penetrated into the soul of the innumerable Chinese who will carry on Jean's spirit and qualities, to further practise Jean's ideals and aspirations, namely, infinite benevolence and boundless love, and build a beautiful world of universal harmony.

Written by: Zhang Baoning, Su Yongqian and Hou Xiaozhe

Data processed by: Wei Lanyu and Yang Chenguang

French data translated by: Jia Baojun and Liu Youyou

Epilogue

Leaders of Xi'an Jiaotong University Health Science Centre and their counterparts at the department of international cooperation and communication, discussing Jean's body donation, 29 September 2015

Jean's friends preparing for the memorial service for Jean, 12 October 2015

A Parisian in Xi'an

Jean's family and friends in the Memorial of Body Donation of Xi'an Jiaotong University Health Science Centre, 13 October 2015

Jean's family in the Memorial of Body Donation of Xi'an Jiaotong University Health Science Centre, 13 October 2015

Epilogue

Jean's former residence in XISU

The memorial service for Jean, and the body donation ceremony, jointly held by XISU and Xi'an Jiaotong University

The memorial service for Jean de Miribel and the body donation ceremony

The body donation monument in Xi'an Jiaotong University Health Science Centre

Vice President Yan Hong of Xi'an Jiaotong University granting the certificate of body donation to Jean's family member, 14 October 2015

Compilers' Notes

On 6 December 2015, the State Council vice premier, and chairman of the Council of Confucius Institute Headquarters, Liu Yandong, related a touching story to all the participants at the opening ceremony of the 10th Confucius Institute conference:

> Here I'd like to share with you the story of a foreign professor known as a 'Chinese good person'. Jean de Miribel, a world famous French scholar, studied and worked in China for 40 years and gave himself a Chinese name, '米睿哲' (Mi Ruizhe). In 1976, he chose to teach in the Xi'an International Studies University (XISU) in north-west China amid harsh conditions, and devoted himself to research and promotion of the Chinese culture, wrote works on the traditional Chinese medicine and the local history of north-west China and delivered outstanding contributions to Sino-French cultural exchanges. He lived a frugal life but subsidised many Chinese students in destitute mountainous regions or studying in France, and accommodated Chinese overseas students in France in his own house in Paris. Professor Jean de Miribel was awarded the French Legion d'Honneur and won the title of 'Person Who Has Performed Good Deeds for China'. He passed away aged 96 in Xi'an on 10 October 2016 and his last wish was to donate his body for medical research. His stories have touched a myriad of Chinese and manifested the unique attraction and enormous power of cultural exchanges. It can be said that the major trend of cultural exchanges, mutual learning and China's progress provided the Confucius Institute with a golden, historic opportunity and platform for development.

The story narrated by vice premier Liu Yandong was sourced from two reports of Gong Shijian, director of the editorial centre of *People's Daily*

Shaanxi branch. In December 2015, the *People's Daily* published Gong Shijian's article '*A Foreign Professor Reputed as a 'Chinese Good Person*''; on 29 February 2016, Gong Shijian reported the meritorious deeds of Jean de Miribel, the late, foreign teacher of XISU, in his article '*Jean de Miribel, A Foreign Professor and A 'Person who has Performed Good Deeds for China' Taking Roots in China for 40 Years and Endeavouring to Stimulate Sino-French Cultural Exchanges During His Lifetime*', in the special section of figures of 'Culture' page in *People's Daily*. On 16 April 2016, China Central Television Education Channel's (CCTV-10) *Story* programme broadcast a feature film entitled *Life of a French Man for China* on French expert at XISU, Jean de Miribel. In the mode of recollections of Jean's students and friends in his lifetime, the programme talked about the moments of Jean's life in XISU and China over 40 years and aroused great attention from all sectors of society. On 15 June, Wang Ping, director of the public utilities editorial office of the People's Publishing House made a special trip to XISU to talk about the compilation and publication of Jean's biography and books and hoped that the XISU and the People's Publishing House would jointly complete the work.

XISU attached great attention to the compilation and publication of Jean's biography and set up the biography compilation group with the university party secretary and the president as the directors, and the deputy party secretary in charge of publicity as the deputy director; the lead group further set up a special office with the director of publicity as the office director and the relevant figures of the department of publicity, the department of international cooperation and communication and the school of French, as well as Jean's friends, specifically in charge of the overall planning and coordination of the biography compilation. At the same time, the university transferred Zhao Pei, Zhang Baoning, Su Yongqian and Wei Lanyu to set up a writing group to write the biography full time. On the afternoon of 19 June, deputy party secretary, Wang Tianping, and party committee member and director of publicity, Duan Henchun held a meeting to initiate the writing on behalf of the biography compilation lead group of the university and required all the compilers to throw themselves into the compilation with a high sense of responsibility and mission, to overcome difficulties with solidarity and cooperation, dig into the deeper implications of Professor Jean de Miribel's moving deeds, try their utmost to enrich the spiritual connotation of the biography, and make positive contributions to telling the stories of XISU.

Compilers' Notes

The members of the writing group began to learn Jean's deeds on 20 June and finished the writing in 15 days, deeply moved by Jean's good deeds during this process as if undergoing a mental baptism. Even the scorching heat in June could not hold off their efforts to explore the spiritual world of the senior French man. Jean was really a man of nobility and purity, divorced from vulgar interests. His sublime personality and lofty spirit aroused people's reverence and they feared that their clumsy narration should fail to present the true stories of Jean. Wang Tianping and Duan Hengchun came to the writing team in person to convey the care for, and the priorities of, their work on behalf of party committee secretary, Deng Zhihui and President Wang Junzhe. They also sent their respects to the compilers, warmly encouraged them and made specific requirements for the writing. The leaders of the department of publicity conducted multilateral coordination, created conditions for the writing group and supported and encouraged the compilers, which moved the compilers and at the same time brought them under more pressure. Chairman of the Labour Union of XISU, Zhao Pei, was busy with his own work but often came to join the writing group in their discussions and drafting efforts. Gong Yuwei assumed the liaison and partial coordination between the compilation lead group office and the compilation group. Geng Qiang and Dang Xiaoxiang worked hard collecting and identifying the photos and data. Lin Zhu, from the foreign affairs office, facilitated the references to Jean's collection of books, lecture notes and books. All these efforts prompted the compilation group to finish the task as required by the organisation.

Zhao Pei made an outline and tried writing Part 1, which was later supplemented and revised by Zhang Baoning. It was discussed by all and approved by the department of publicity of the university party committee. According to the new outline, the introduction and conclusion were written by Zhang Baoning, Chapter 1 and Chapter 2 by Su Yongqian, and Chapters 3-6 by Hou Xiaozhe. Finally, Zhang Baoning was responsible for compiling and drawing up the title and subtitles of all the chapters of the book and drafted the 'Editors' Notes'; Wei Lanyu took the responsibility of classifying and printing the materials for interview and information discussion; Jia Baojun and Liu Youyou translated and classified the French data; Dong Yang interviewed the vice chairman, Hu Sishe of Chinese People's Association for Friendship with Foreign Countries. During the writing, they successively held informal discussions with Jean's colleagues, students and friends, including Ren Zhanfeng, Huang Chuangen, Sun Lijian, Geng Qiang, Yang Chenguang, Li Tao, Zhang Cheng, Ren Yanfang,

Qiu Changqin, Xing Zhiqiang and Cui Shengrui. Jia Zhenfan and Zhang Ping offered recollections of Jean in writing, and numerous friends of Jean also wrote down their recollections in the WeChat group, all of which provided abundant, lively material for the writing of this book. The writing references the articles of Lu Dong, Wang Kejian, Ren Zhanfeng, Liang Jialin, Jiang Xiaomin, Zhu Weimin, Wang Liqun and Zhao Chengxun etc, written in memory of Jean and refer to the autograph album *Jean de Miribel, the Love of a Senior French Man for China*, in honour of Jean, and the two articles '*Missing the Envoy of Love, Jean de Miribel*' and '*A Good Senior French Man: Great Love Surpassing the Length of Life*' written by Lu Dong and Liu Hairong, respectively, and published in *Charity Focus*, the 12th issue of 2015. Comrades Guo Futing, Gong Yuwei and Dang Xiaoxiang, with the party committee publicity department of XISU, under the arrangement and instructions of director Duan Hengchun, spent more than two years carefully collecting and meticulously classifying the life story and text-and-image data of Jean, from May 2014. Guo Futing successively wrote news reports on Jean's deeds entitled *"A Peaceful Life of a 'Model Man' - a 'Chinese Good Person' from France"* and *"The Alive Not Losing Their Spirit Can Live Longer and the Dead Not Losing Their Spirit Can Enjoy Longevity – Meritorious Deeds of Mr. Jean de Miribel, a 'Model Chinese'"* which totalled more than 13,000 characters, and cooperated with the CCTV Education Channel to complete the filming of a feature documentary on Jean de Miribel during the winter of 2016. All the previous work laid a solid foundation for the compilation and writing of this book. Without the help of the aforesaid people and literature, this book could not have been finished and heartfelt thanks should go to them. The narration in the book might not have detailed all Jean's good deeds, his thoughts and spirit. It is hoped that more, better stories of China and Jean can be written with inspiration from Jean's spirit.

The compilation group
Xi'an International Studies University
5 July 2016

Jean de Miribel

(1919-2015)

Told by Jean's Family

To explain Jean's life and understand him, we cannot relate his stories without placing him in the history of his family. During World War II (WWII), half of the territory of France was occupied by the Nazi troops but Jean served in the Youth Workshops, a kind of unarmed military service for two years. The military camp was quartered at the neighbouring commune of Miribel Lanchatre, home of his family, and he often came back home on foot.

The surname of 'Miribel' originated from the Latin expression 'mire bellum', meaning 'beautiful sight' and referred to the exceptional site on a promontory 20km south of Grenoble where two strong castles were built in succession. The first was built by Humbertus de Miribel, around 1000 and donated to Benedictine monastery in 1030.

Quickly, the second castle was built not far away, with a chapel dedicated to Saint Martin. The first castle collapsed in ruins in 1789 and the second was burnt down a few years later during the French Revolution. Jean never claimed the honour of this ancient heritage but he was perfectly aware of the exemplary value given by a lineage that had gone through the vicissitudes of history. It was indeed this example that Jean would apply with intransigence to himself throughout his life.

A family history in the service of France and some family personages closer to Jean also influenced Jean's life.

The first one was Jean's grandfather, named Joseph de Miribel (1831-1893) who successively acted as the general of a division and chief of staff of the armies. After the heavy defeat of France by Germany in 1870, he reorganised the French armies. In addition, his orders for mobilisation were to be implemented in 1914...

The site of Miribel with the ruins of the old castle

As Jean recounted, his grandfather's military exploits were significantly influential in Germany. During WWII, the German military officers found Joseph's son, Fernand de Miribel, hiding a Jewish woman in his house in Savoy. Out of respect for his father, the chief of staff, who had departed 50 years before, he was not deported to the concentration camp. Jean's sister, Jacqueline, then opened the door for the two German officers. She can still remember the episode, and the look of the Jewish woman during her departure for the camps.

General Joseph de Miribel

Joseph de Miribel had his own family home at the Châtelard in Hauterives in Dauphiné, France. A statue was erected in the heart of the village in his honour. Jean's parents liked to go to the home with its warm atmosphere. Jean had never seen his grandfather. Nevertheless, his grandfather's integrity, self-discipline and uprightness shown in a difficult period for France were manifested in Jean, his grandson. Jean's father, Fernand de Miribel, (1847-1967) was also a soldier, graduating from the Ecole Polytechnique (1898) and joining the army, first in the artillery, and then as a pilot of surveillance aircraft. Endowed with a lively intelligence and a great finesse, he was discreet, humble and demanding of himself and his relatives. He encouraged each of his children on their own way.

Fernand de Miribel, Jean's father, beside his airplane in 1916

Jean de Miribel's aunt, Marie de Miribel (1872-1959), was the elder sister of Jean's father. When she was young, she felt pain at the sight of the poor in the slums and the patients and children to be rescued in the eastern districts of Paris. Although well-to-do, she decided to become a nurse and persuaded many of her friends to contribute to charity. In the early 20th century, she organised a social welfare centre and opened a care home which became what is today a large hospital in eastern Paris, the 'St Simeon's Cross'. Marie de Miribel once wrote: "The aim of the social services is to supplement the work of the physician whose role is to diagnose and treat diseases, to assist people in all fields with advice and encouragement and to take all necessary steps." She refused all the glories and set her own motto: "Honour, not honour"... This attention for the most deprived, the love of the weak, the vision to establish a hospital from nothing but perseverance were also the traits shown in Jean. It was just for this reason that Jean built the bridge of friendship with the ATD Fourth World organisation (the association set up jointly by Geneviève de Gaulle and Germaine Tillion to help people in difficulties).

His cousin, Élisabeth de Miribel (1915-2005), typed General de Gaulle's *18 June 1940 Appeal*[1] speech, delivered on 18 June 1940. She then completed numerous missions during WWII including as a press correspondent. Failing to become a nun, she continued to serve France as a diplomat. Her determined character, extensive knowledge and volunteering were a real point of intellectual reference for Jean.

Marie de Miribel

---

[1] **French title: *L'Appel du 18 Juin***

In her book *Freedom Suffers Violence*[2], published in 1981, she reflects on that day in June 1940 when *The 18 June 1940 Appeal* was typed. "On the afternoon of 17 June 1940, after a long wait, the phone finally rang. I was told to come to a small apartment on the Seymour plaza the following morning. Sitting before a typewriter, I had difficulty deciphering the handwritten sheets. To save time, Geoffroy de Courcel dictated the passages to me. He took away the typewritten sheets and submitted them to General de Gaulle time and again. These words would constitute a page of history, but I did not know it then. Nevertheless, I had an obscure presentiment that I was participating in an exceptional event."

Françoise de Fréville (1892-1987) was the tender mother Jean deeply loved. Mother of six children, she was cheerful and lively, intelligent and well cultivated, always ready to listen. She was born in a simple, unsophisticated environment and lived a comfortable life, destroyed by wars. She deliberately looked to the future and encouraged her descendants to realise their own plans. For that reason, wherever he was, Jean would travel each year to France to find her, share with her and be nourished by her love. Jean liked to join his cousins on his mother's side and play tennis with them in the city of Livet in Normandy.

Élisabeth de Miribel in 1940

---

[2] French title: *La Liberté Souffre Violence*

Jean de Miribel's newly-wed parents

Jean liked to go on holiday with his uncle, his mother's brother-in-law, Jean d'Aillères in his house in La Pelice. Married and without children, well-cultivated and able to speak Latin fluently, his uncle recited to Jean whole pages from great authors, and was especially passionate, like Jean, about the history of France. For Jean, it was the starting point of his new horizons that led him towards his passion for geopolitics and the play of powers through history and the world.

Jean's family circle in his youth made an impression on him. Jean was loyal to them throughout his life, often referring to them as his friends, and he took them as guides or examples.

Jean spent his early years in a house at 12, Rue Cassette, in the sixth arrondissement of Paris, with his parents, servants and a circle of relations. Each night, his aunt, Marie de Miribel joined her brother's family for dinner. Only the elder children, including Jean and his sister Bernadette were allowed to join in the conversations, and had to return to their own rooms after dinner, leaving the adults to continue in the living room. Jacqueline said: "As early as 1930, Bernadette, Gérard and Philippe were boarders. Only Catherine and I stayed at home, spending four and seven years with Jean respectively. We went to our rooms after dinner every evening: Jean at the end of the corridor, and my sister and I in our shared room."

A family life as we know it today, with six children playing together, was not what Jean lived. The eldest son of the family (Jean, Bernadette, Gérard, Jacqueline, Philippe and Catherine – all but Jacqueline and Catherine had the chance to spend a long time in Asia), he was their playmate and was much loved and esteemed by his younger brothers and sisters! Afterwards, Jean developed deep, heart-to-heart relations with each of them, which grew stronger with the passage of time. Considerate and careful, Jean wanted to be attentive to everyone even when the distance created a definitive separation, with his permanent settlement in China.

Jean de Miribel's parents (in Beauregard)

From left to right: Bernadette, Gérard, Philippe, Madame de Miribel, Catherine, Jacqueline and Jean In 1927

He studied at the Lycée Montaigne and then at the Lycée Louis le Grand, where he was a studious and curious pupil. This did not prevent him from teasing and playing many pranks on his sisters Jacqueline and Catherine in his capacity as the eldest son of the family. As his sister Jacqueline told: "He said 'Hurry up, it's seven o'clock, you have to get up!' I got out of my bed, half-asleep, went on the landing, and realised that Jean was teasing me, and it always worked with me!" He kept this humour, as reported by his brother Gérard, on his return from Xi'an in 2005: "Lu Dong and his wife, I and my wife dined with Jean in a superb restaurant in an enclosed room with a canopy, as in the days of the mandarins. Jean suddenly transformed the de Miribel couple into mandarins, provoking general hilarity, and Jean was bent double in laughter at this spectacle!"

Jean was a cheerful child and one sees him with a smile in his pictures as a child, as well as a head taller than his brothers and sisters… He was the tall, eldest son of the family. They could still clearly remember his readiness to help others, especially his brother and sisters with their studies…

At his father's retirement in 1938, the family settled in Grenoble, then in 1942, during the war, in a house in Beauregard, Savoie, which Jean found for his parents during a bicycle ride. In Grenoble, Jean passed a history exam before being mobilised. When he served in the Youth Workshops, he did not hesitate in the middle of winter "to surprise us with a family reunion in Grenoble, where he arrived with a toe all black, frozen after a 20km walk" recalled Jacqueline... This region with its mountains attracted Jean to the high peaks that he had known during holidays in Switzerland in 1935. With friends, from the age of 15, he climbed higher and higher and became a good climber: there was Mont-Blanc of course, but also the Dru and the Aiguille Verte, where he trained his brother, Gérard. Beauregard brought the opportunity to multiply these escapades and his sister Catherine still retains all the emotion and pride of the ascent of 4000m under his leadership, and "the joy of his father when he returned, questioning him so that Jean told him the snow, the glaciers, the summits, the superb views of the Alps!"

Jean, Bernadette, Gérard, Amédée (a cousin), Catherine, Philippe and Jacqueline

Jean was seriously ill when he was very young and recovered thanks to the care, attentions and prayers of his parents, especially his mother. That episode certainly marked him because he quickly adopted the idea of filling his life with meaning...

The war broke out suddenly. Jean was mobilised and joined the camp in Avord and then a school of officer cadets, installed in Fontenay-le-Comte. In the disorganisation that reigned, he crossed France in search of his assignment and was taken prisoner. It is during this experience of war, in the face of the helplessness of the abandoned soldiers and the multiple sufferings of the families, wandering and displaced, while seeing the differences in fate related to education or social environments, that he made the voluntary choice to consecrate his life to the weak and the oppressed, wishing to live among them, with what nourished him internally.

For this reason, he began his long studies on the spiritual philosophical level in Issy- les-Moulineaux. He committed himself to serving the poorest and the deprived, without becoming involved in the religious considerations, in Lisieux in 1946. From then on, he never wanted to promote his status, wishing to live from his work and to testify his spiritual commitment by the example of his life.

In the same year, he settled at 27, Rue du Moulin de la Pointe, in the 13th arrondissement of Paris (now the China quarter in Paris) and lived by doing a little job as a postcard gilder. His door was always open, overlooking the passage... One came, one passed and one chatted... His neighbours, whoever they were, were all his friends, even the prisoners just out of prison.

In 1953, he moved to a place near Avenue d'Italie.

Far away from his aristocratic life and among the destitute, Jean lived a simple, adventurous life, in Paris from 1949 to 1962, in Brazil from 1964 to 1968, where he learned of his father's death in 1967, and then in Hong Kong from 1969 to 1976. He lived in China from 1976.

Each time, he made the effort to retrain professionally to earn a living. He worked as a fisherman and made TV sets (he gave the first TV he made to his mother), learned Portuguese, Cantonese and Mandarin (he already knew German through his studies) and began to use a computer and then the internet when he was in his eighties. He took advantage of each change of course to enrich himself with discoveries, to learn about non-violence in Brazil, or to travel extensively in the United States, which he did not know, when he returned from Brazil. His discoveries and incessant learning were not superficial: in addition to learning different languages, he established close ties with people of different countries and immersed himself in a new culture, and humbly sought to apprehend all its finesse. This brought with it his usual demands of all sorts of preparatory work, or minute preparation of meetings, travels, negotiations, subjects of study, whether for himself or for those he helped. In China, he opened his thesis to the universe of medicine and earned the friendship and recognition of many famous physicians including Professor Guy de Thé. In the opposite direction, he successfully sent more than 40 young Chinese to perfect their studies in languages or medicine in France or elsewhere, and accommodated and subsidised them.

Jean, in his nineties, in front of the computer

Jean threw himself into his arduous life, struggling to help everyone live with dignity. In Paris, he engaged in his first fights, sometimes rough, without complacency or compromise with the same exigency for himself as for the others. At the ceremony held for Jean on 28 November 2015, in his old quarter of the 13th arrondissement in Paris, it was striking to see how the friendships born there almost 60 years ago were still perennial, rooted in common struggles, friendliness always nourished by Jean since Xi'an. Thus Geneviève Collas testified: "Jean was always attentive to others, especially to those whom nobody noticed. They were all unforgettable experiences. What a joy to have had the chance to rub shoulders with such a being! Later, when I resumed contact with him in China, I was overwhelmed by the way he spoke about the charity of the Chinese people."

A few weeks before his death, he had been bedridden. He hummed for those around him the song for the Auvergnat of Georges Brassens:

> *This song is for you,*
> *You, the Auvergnat who, without manner,*
> *Gave me four pieces of wood.*
> *When it was cold in my life,*
> *You gave me the fire when*
> *Crunchy and crunchy,*
> *And all well-meaning people,*
> *Had locked the door to my nose...*

Recalling the lyrics, he added that the songwriters of that period wrote texts with a meaning close to the reality of the people that lived in the 13th arrondissement in Paris.

His sister Bernadette accompanied him. She had learned Chinese in Hong Kong, which was useful to help Jean type his doctoral dissertation *Asian Research on Provincial Administration and Civil Servants in the Ming Dynasty (1368-1644): Study of Shaanxi Province and Xi'an Prefecture*, of more than 700 pages (Chinese edition), and lived among the poverty-stricken people in the damp, sultry ship, during their passage. Then she went to Lebanon and Syria, to Afghanistan, and then to Egypt, learning Arabic and living a similar life there. To Jean, she was a fellow traveller, his harbour, his secretary and his beloved sister, despite a long distance between them. They had kept up a strong friendship nourished by abundant correspondence.

Both chose to renounce the material inheritance of their parents in order to remain free from the delights of money, only wanting to live by their own work.

Thus began the life of Jean, in a family nourished with a history linked to that of France, surrounded by the unfailing love of his brothers and sisters whom he would think of so often, and already at the heart of a network of friendships traversing all the strata of the French society, a network which he would not cease to extend across country and universe. Although his permanent settlement in China marked a break in the possibility of encounters, he tried to remain connected with all these relations and friendships until his last days in China.

From 1964 to 1968, Jean spent more than three years in São Paulo, an immense city, and almost two in Belem, at the mouth of the Amazon. He embarked in Le Havre, after having learned in the evening of a new job as a TV engineer. A fracture to the neck of his femur meant a stay in several hospitals, where he discovered the faith of the poor. It was in Brazil that he discovered medicine, by working in a laboratory of medical biology.

Jean returned from Brazil in August 1968, after a long journey by coach via Panama, the United States and Canada. Catherine remembered: "Jean returned. What a joy! We had not seen him in five years! He told us all about Brazil... and already he thought of China... Without talking about it, would it be a thought that had not left him since his youth?" Brazil was for him a necessary step before China, of which he had long thought. One of his friends, Michel Grolleaud recounted an interview he had with Jean about this as early as 1964!

A Parisian in Xi'an

Jean, and his little sister Bernadette, in the house of their parents in Beauregard

It was in January 1969 that Jean left for Hong Kong, where he arrived on 15 March 1969, to prepare for the country he wanted to begin. Along the way, he had the joy of meeting Mother Theresa in Calcutta, India.

Commenting on his plan to go to China, she encouraged him with these simple words: "The good grain piled up, rots!" meaning that Europe had already benefited from many men like him...

Catherine said: "Jean learned Chinese while being a French teacher at the Alliance Française. At 50, he began to learn Chinese! There too, there would be some friends. With Roger, my husband, we went to see him, for the first time, to know the Asian land... a great discovery. We felt so happy about his approach to the Chinese world. He spent seven years in Hong Kong." He was enrolled in New Asia College, an institution partnered with Yale University, at which he would follow the courses of Mandarin and Chinese civilisation for several years.

In late 1975, Jean knew that he could teach in a university in China. So he set off for the first time on a trip to Beijing, Dalian, Qingdao and Shanghai in July 1976 at the age of 57. In Beijing, he was invited to parade past the remains of Chairman Mao Zedong. The terrible Tangshan earthquake hit China on 28 July and Jean was deeply affected by the sufferings of the Chinese. He joined XISU (Xi'an International Studies University) on 21

Jean just arriving in Hong Kong in 1969

September 1976 and taught there from that day on! He did not leave the city where he spent almost 40 years...

He had made another long departure without telephone or internet! He did, however, visit his mother in Beauregard when he returned to France each year. He travelled back and forth between Asia and France and took new routes crossing India, Pakistan, Afghanistan, Iran, Iraq, Syria or Russia with the Siberian railway. He even made a detour through Japan and witnessed, in Hiroshima, the horror of the atomic war.

Jean invited his three sisters and his brother, Philippe, on a four-week cultural trip to China with his friends in October 1980. Catherine said: "we discovered China and the life of the Chinese, the bicycle culture of the whole population... the old quarters, the life in the country... Beijing, the Forbidden City, Temple of Heaven, Great Wall and the Ming Tombs. We were sumptuously received by the Director of the University, the professors and all those who knew Jean, realising how happy he was in the midst of his pupils and friends. What a wonderful memory... The scene that Jean bid farewell to us at the foot of the airplane is still vivid in our mind today... my heart was tight then. We told everything to our mother who was waiting for us with impatience."

1986 marked the recognition of 10 years' of work by Jean, under the

A Parisian in Xi'an

tutelage of Professor Léon Vandermeersch, with the presentation of his thesis, at Paris Diderot University, in the presence of two professors from China, Guo Taichu and Lu Dong. His family was also present, his mother in particular, was passionate about these encounters with the Chinese.

There were many testimonies of westerners, such as that of Olivier Rol: "He was an extraordinary messenger of emotions and ideas, with vision and the ultimate goal of narrowing the distance between east and west, which we know so badly, to our detriment." He added: "Throughout his years in China, he touched so many people."

During all these years in China, Jean wanted to create a bridge of friendship between China and France, two countries of great culture, he said. He knew the French culture fairly well and was also immersed in the Chinese culture. In the city which used to be the capital city, historically, he made many contacts and launched initiatives, often long and lengthy efforts, without ever despairing. He hoped his native country could better grasp these opportunities and build the bridge of friendship between the peoples of the countries he loved.

The above tells Jean's origins, his family and the birth of his project in China. China, a country to which he no doubt thought of going in his youth, was delighted to receive him, and more than 30 years later gave him the honour of welcoming him for his retirement. In France, his own family understood that for Jean, for a long time, his second country was China and his beloved family was in China, with many loved ones. He said that he had learned a great deal from his friends in China, often seeing them as an example of devotion and attention to the weak. At his end of life in his apartment, he was surrounded daily, sometimes day and night, by his companions and young students of his first days in Xi'an. Isn't it a perfect illustration? The family of Jean would like to thank each of them warmly.

What follows should be written by the Chinese people who knew and loved Jean, to describe his extraordinary personality, his character marked by endless tenacity, intelligence, hard work, networks of relationships, self-denial and help for those with whom he lived...

Professor Lu Dong and Jean's mother, during Jean's doctoral dissertation presentation, in France in 1986

His face was always animated by an intense gaze, which will be remembered by those who knew him, as well as his smile, and his passionate tirades animated with large reels of his right hand or index finger, firmly pointing forward! Ma Qing recalls Jean as: "Without any pretence, yet full of eloquence, with his modesty and sense of humility, yet full of compassion and love of humanity, his mind was exceptionally clear, but simply accessible, full of courage and the sacrifice of his life".

What on earth made him live this far from his roots? What nourished his intense and varied friendships? It was his attention to everyone and the strength of his character that overcame all obstacles. His real feelings for everyone near him were a mystery... He lived like a poor man but 'served those who needed to be loved'.

Jean, newly arrived in Xi'an

A Parisian in Xi'an

It is through these words that we find the whole unity of his life, isn't it?

Jean reading in China

Jean de Miribel

Jean is remembered for his smile

Chronology – Jean de Miribel

5 August 1919:

Born in Paris

1929 to 1937:

Secondary studies in Paris at Lycée Montaigne and then at Lycée Louis le Grand

1939:

Obtained bachelor of history degree in Grenoble

April 1940:

Mobilised

September 1940:

Assigned to the 9th grouping of the Youth Workshops

September 1942:

Demobilised and continued studies

From July 1946 to 1960:

In the 13th arrondissement of Paris, as a priest and worker

1960:

Decided to serve outside France and became a TV editor in Montreuil

1961:

Trainee at Notre Dame des Champs and then at Oceanic in Courbevoie

1964:

Destination Brazil; Jean learned Portuguese during the crossing in a freighter

1964 to 1967:

São Paolo, Brazil

28 December 1967:

Death of Jean's father

1967 to 1968:

Worked in a laboratory of medical biology in Belem, Brazil

February to August 1968:

Return via South America, the United States and Canada

15 March 1969:

Arrived in Hong Kong after a long journey by land and sea from Europe

1969 to 1976:

Resided in Hong Kong, began to learn Cantonese, gave courses at the Alliance Française and enrolled in New Asia College

July 1976:

Made his first trip to China, following the terrible Tangshan earthquake

September 1976:

Invited to parade past the remains of Chairman Mao Zedong

21 September 1976:

Joined XISU

October 1980:

His three sisters, a brother and a sister-in-law visited him in Xi'an and made a four-week cultural journey there prepared by Jean

1985:

Retired

1986:

Doctoral dissertation presented in Paris Diderot University on *Asian Research on Provincial Administration and Civil Servants in the Ming Dynasty (1368-1644): Study of Shaanxi Province and Xi'an Prefecture*, a monumental work of more than 1,000 pages (French edition)

14 November 1987:

Death of his mother, Françoise de Fréville de Lorme

5 May 1994:

Awarded the Legion d'Honneur, presented by the French Ambassador in Xi'an

1997:

Shaanxi province granted him permanent residence permit in China: Jean decided to stay in China until the end of his days

2000:

Made his last trip in France

September 2013:

Decided to donate his body to Chinese medicine

10 May 2014:

Was named "Person Who Has Performed Good Deeds for China' by Shaanxi province

January 2015:

Granted the 'Person Who Performs Good Deeds for China' certificate by the Central Civilisation Office of the People's Republic of China

10 October 2015:

Died in Xi'an

14 October 2015:

Memorial ceremony with the authorities of XISU and Xi'an Jiaotong University Health Science Centre

18 October 2015:

XISU decided to dedicate a place in the new campus to the work of Jean

28 November 2015:

Memorial ceremony in honour of Jean in the 13th arrondissement in Paris